Because You Can

DO THE THING YOU WANT TO DO EVEN IF IT FEELS IMPOSSIBLE

DANIEL STIH

Copyright ©2025 by Daniel Stih

All rights reserved.

ISBN 978-1-7365856-3-4

This is the second edition, updated with a new subtitle and preface.

No part of this book may be reproduced or transmitted in any form, electronic or mechanical, including photocopying, without written permission from the author, except for brief passages in a magazine or newspaper review.

Inquiries regarding requests to reprint parts should be addressed to the publisher at:

369 Montezuma Ave #169
Santa Fe, NM 87501

WARNING!

If this book was a story about climbing Mt. Everest and after reading it you attempted to climb Everest, I hope you would not blame me if you lost your toes to frostbite. This book contains the principles and beliefs I applied to climb mountains that had previously not been climbed by anyone. Do not apply them to situations that could be dangerous. These are principles. Consider them colors of the rainbow. **Don't try to jump over the rainbow to grab the pot of gold without additional help, counseling, or consulting.**

Dedicated to Nick

To the unseen force I know as my guardian angel. You've guided me through challenges, helped me find the path when it seemed unclear, and kept me safe in moments I can't explain. And to whatever unseen hands or forces have helped along the way—whether you call them chance, intuition, higher intelligence, or simply grace—thank you. I've felt the presence of support beyond my own, and I'm grateful for it.

Table of Contents

It Happens	5
Do What Interests You	15
Be Where You Are	27
Extract Yourself	41
Discover the Truth	53
Luck Favors the Prepared	67
Ask for Help	85
Expect a Few Bumps	91
Take Your Opportunities	101
Start	115
Believe in Yourself	121
Fear Just Means Think Twice	139
What If	153
Trust the Heart to Work with the Head	157
Be Flexible	173
Take Risks	189
If You Keep Going You Will Get There	203
Be Thankful	217
You Can Have More Then One Dream	225
Creating Your Roadmap to Success	227

Preface

Why Doing the Thing You Want to Do Is the Solution to Everything

Most people don't realize how many of the world's problems begin with one simple fact: too many people are not doing the thing they want to do. They're working jobs they don't care about. They're holding back ideas, songs, businesses, books — because of fear, doubt, or what someone else might think. They're doing what's expected; not what feels alive.

When people live like that — disconnected from who they really are — the effects ripple out. We over consume as we are unfulfilled. We lash out because we feel trapped. We vote for control because we feel powerless. We start wars on the outside as there's a war inside us.

I believe the most radical thing you can do, for yourself and the world, is to do the thing you truly want to do, instead of the thing that looks good on a résumé. Not the thing that makes the most money. The thing that calls to you. The thing you'd do if no one clapped. That's what

Because You Can

this book is about.

The stories I share are from my time climbing, including mountains no one had ever climbed. This book, however, is not about climbing. It's about waking up, stepping into fear, and moving forward. It's about succeeding —not by following a formula — by following yourself.

If more people were doing what they were meant to do — what they wanted to do - we'd have fewer angry people, fewer broken systems, fewer power-hungry leaders. We'd have more creativity, more contribution, more peace. You don't have to change the whole world. Just stop ignoring your part in it.

Let's Be Clear

When I say "Do the thing you want to do," I don't mean it's OK to be rude, loud, or insensitive. I'm not promoting selfishness or recklessness disguised as authenticity. Rather, I believe in kindness, being thoughtful and respectful of others, even when you disagree. This book isn't a license to ignore decency. It's a reminder to stop ignoring yourself. I don't believe in censorship. I believe in common sense. Speak your truth. Speak it like someone who knows they're part of something bigger.

Doing the thing you want to do may not be easy. It's not always convenient, comfortable and risk-free. I got my engineering degree while working full time and still

Preface

made time to go climbing. I risked losing my job to pursue what mattered.

This book isn't about wishful thinking or waiting for perfect conditions. It's about knowing how to move forward even when there are obstacles. And there will be. It's about recognizing those obstacles don't have to stop you. Most people wait until everything is lined up just right. That moment may never come. Do it anyway — because you can.

Why This Changes Everything

How will this change the world? Doing the thing you want to do disrupts what's expected of you. It makes you unpredictable. Unpredictability makes it harder to control someone or something. Systems of control rely on routine behavior, fear, and people staying in their boxes.

When you start doing what lights you up, you're no longer easy to manipulate. You feel better, positive, alive. In New Age terms, you have a "higher vibration." In practical terms, you are happier. You treat others better. People who are lit up from within don't waste their time trying to dim others. You'll certainly be better off than if you do not do the thing you want to do. The more people who step into this kind of life, the freer, healthier, more creative this world will become.

Because You Can

Preface

So read this book with your thing in mind — the one you've been putting off, hiding from, or pretending it doesn't matter.

Because it does.
And you can.

— Daniel

Because You Can

Introduction

Mountain climbing - our evolutionary journey - is fraught with difficulty. But the climb makes us stronger, wiser, and more deeply human. And the higher we go, the more beautiful the view, because we begin to view our lives in perspective, until finally we see the bigger picture, the many faces of God.
- Dan Millman, Author, *The Life you Were Born to Live*

This is not a book about climbing. It's a book about self-improvement, setting goals, and achieving them. Ultimately, it's about creating the life we want for ourselves. The principles presented in this book can be applied to any situation that requires getting over an obstacle and reaching a goal. It might be that your business needs to make changes to have a better year. It might be a personal challenge such as winning a battle with a diagnosis affecting your health. For me, one struggle was getting through college. I got a degree in aerospace engineering while working full time in a factory.

I am not a professional climber and have never been

Because You Can

sponsored. I'm not the best, fastest, or strongest climber. Following the principles in this book empowered me to achieve things I could never have imagined, such as scaling mountains that had never previously been climbed. My claim to fame is climbing thirty mountains (as of today) that had never been climbed by anyone else, ten of which are labeled on maps of the United States.

I hope my stories encourage you to follow your dream and do what you believe will make you happy. I'm humbled by the opportunity to share my stories with you. The thought crossed my mind: Who am I to write a book on motivation and success just because I climbed some mountains that had not been climbed? I know some of you have real problems.

What makes me qualified is the simple fact that I have done things no one else was able to do. I've been successful where others failed. My success was not a one-time, one-hit wonder. It seems I have a recipe, a system and method for success. Referring to *The 7 Habits of Successful People*, someone asked me to write my principles down. The chapters in the Table of Contents are what I came up with.

Each chapter in this book covers a principle, followed by a story in which I used the principle to succeed. The principles are in the order as might be needed to overcome a challenge, the order you might encounter or require them on your road to success. Depending on

Introduction

your circumstance, not all of them may apply.

At the end of selected chapters you will find tips on how a principle can be used to transform uncertainty into taking action to move ahead. These are provided for quick reference when you find yourself uncertain about how to proceed on your quest for success. To help you succeed, I've also developed a method for creating a roadmap to success. At the end of select chapters, there are steps and suggestions for creating your roadmap. I suggest doing these exercises. The process is summarized in the final chapter, which includes a flow chart on how the pieces and principles fit together.

I focus on climbing mountains because that is my passion. Most likely, it is not yours. You will not be happy pursuing the goals and passions of others. You might be passionate about watching college football. You might think you can't follow that passion any further because you can't be a player. If watching is your passion, then you can be an announcer or do something in the industry.

The principles I present in this book can be used to solve and overcome challenges in different walks of life. I've used them to achieve success. It's your turn. Use them to climb your mountains, whatever they may be.

Because You Can

This book was ready go to print when the following happened and I realized it wasn't complete. I didn't do anything wrong. If I had a chance, I might do things the same. Sometimes it happens.

It Happens

It's not what happens to you, but how you react to it that matters.
- Epictetus

Because You Can

Laying flat on my back, looking up at the helicopter hovering above me and the cable swinging below it, I wondered, *what does this mean for me? How will I come back from this?*

I overhead one of the search and rescue team members counting off the hazards to the pilot: "...trees, blowing debris, rock fall..."

"Do you have sunglasses?" the EMT asked me.

I understood and put my sunglasses on. The helicopter slowly lowered until it was forty feet above us. Confident it could hover that close, it re-gained altitude and flew away.

I started climbing in 1983. Since then I've never had a serious accident. At the time of writing, I'd been climbing in Zion thirty years. I knew the mountains well. On this trip I had the best partner I could ask for. He was in his twenties, strong, and got out on a regular basis. We carried 600 feet of special, lightweight rope. The plan was to climb all of the Beehives, a series of peaks on the tops of mountains, some which had never been climbed, and finish by going down the canyons between them, something that had not been done before.

The day before, things had looked great. We had been climbing for three days and had been successful in climbing all of the beehives. We were going down the last canyon, and were only 400 feet to reach the ground.

It Happens

When Mike, my partner, commented on how precarious things seemed, I said there was no way that anything bad could happen to us. I smiled and said, "I'll go first."

I should have gone down straight, but the cliff below looked blank. So I descended diagonally, on terrain littered with bushes. My logic was, if I came to the end of my rope, I could use one of the bushes for an anchor.

Suddenly I heard a branch snap. The rope, unknown to me, had been running over a bush. I found myself swinging like a pendulum. I tried to keep my feet moving across the face of the rock to prevent twisting an ankle. I felt a G-force, and thought, *wow, I'm moving pretty fast.* I swung around a corner just in time to see a wall facing my left side. I came to an immediate and complete stop, as the side of my hip slammed into the wall.

Fortunately I found myself at a small ledge. I unclipped from the rope and slumped onto it. I felt sharp pains from nerves and ligaments. My foot felt tingly, and didn't move in the direction I wished it. I didn't yet know that I had broken the ball in my hip bone in half, and a piece had lowered. It was going to be difficult to get to the ground. We had to get to the ground.

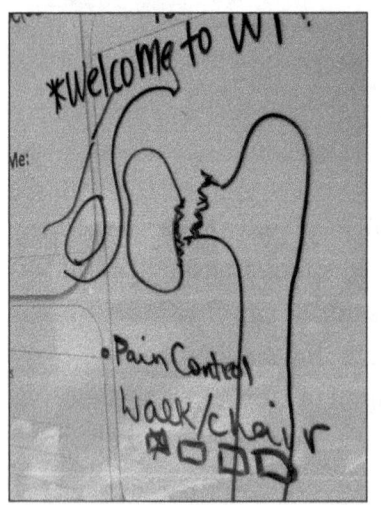

You have to stand up, I thought.

I imagined myself as a football player, injured on the field, willing himself to get up. I imagined getting up, and then by some miracle, running around the stadium, dancing as the crowd cheered.

I was unsuccessful.

I replayed the movie in my head. *Got to stand up Dan. You have to do it.*

I used our trekking poles like crutches, to get on my feet, and making sure my bad leg did not touch anything. Mike then lowered me, inch by inch, to the

It Happens

bottom of the mountain. I got lucky. I landed in a small patch of sand in the otherwise rocky moat.

When Mike got down I said, "Just leave me. Go for help."

It was late in the day and I assumed it would be tomorrow before I was rescued. I was surprised therefore, when, an hour before dark, I head voices. It was Mike, followed by two members of the search and rescue (SAR) team.

Because You Can

The team assessed it was too dangerous to move me, since the femur artery is close to the hip. If I cut an artery, I'd bleed to death. They decided to have a helicopter extract me in the morning. They said if I didn't think I could make it until morning, they could call a Black Hawk helicopter and get me out that night. I told them I could wait. I tossed and turned all night long, trying to find a position that lessened the pain. I didn't get any sleep.

The helicopter returned, this time, hauling a man on a cable through the air. It slowly lowered itself until the man was standing next to me. He unclipped from the cable and the helicopter flew away. He had brought with him an inflatable litter. I rolled on to the litter and got into a comfortable position with my knees bent. I found it hurt more if my legs were straight. Once I was in position, the team used a hand pump to blow it so I was "packaged," then called for the helicopter to come back.

I hadn't taken any medication for pain, and wondered what would happen if, when the helicopter lifted me into the air, my leg started hurting. What choice did I have? I was clipped to it, lifted into the air, and whisked away. Fortunately, I was comfortable. The parking lot of a nearby hotel had been cleared for my landing. The copter gently lowered me to waiting hands. After being unclipped from the cable and removed from the litter packaging, with the help from two shoulders to lean on,

It Happens

I hobbled to Mike's van and he drove me to the hospital. I waived taking an ambulance. I didn't have insurance.

The surgeon decided it was better to fix my bones with screws, than give me a new hip. The surgery went well. The day after surgery I left the hospital with a walker. I still had pains running down my thigh, and black-and-blue marks behind my knee, as if I'd stretched and torn strings and muscles, ones not fixed by surgery.

I wasn't worried. I was grateful.

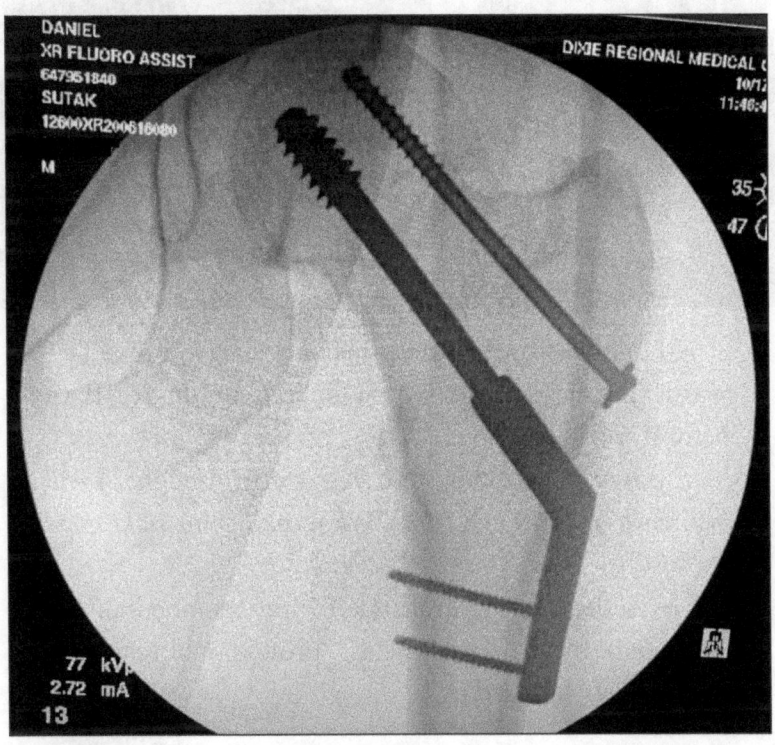

Because You Can

Two weeks later, I returned to see my surgeon. I stayed in a hotel near the mountains. My morning ritual was eating pancakes at the restaurant next door. I had trouble sleeping, so I was up early. One morning, as I went to get breakfast I found the restaurant was burning down.

No one was hurt. I took this as a sign to move forward. The restaurant would be rebuilt, better than before, and so would I.

This is an opportunity for a fresh start, I thought. *It will be months before I can climb. What can I do to make good use of this time?*

I have the deepest gratitude for the members of the SAR team. It was a world-class, professional rescue of the highest standard.

It Happens

Takeaway

Sometimes things go wrong even for the best of us. It will be OK. Don't dwell on how or why it happened. Just get up and move forward.

As you read the rest of the stories in this book, particularly, the final chapter, "Be Thankful", you will see why I believe there are no accidents. I think the mountains and my angels were conspiring together. The bush didn't drink enough water that season so that it would be dry enough, and helpers pushed me like I was on a swing, as my Guardian Angel ensured that I landed in the right spot and got only what I needed (a broken hip), and nothing more. I didn't hurt my head or die from bleeding.

Because You Can

Do What Interests You

When you choose the path in your heart, a door will open.
- Unknown

As I was graduating from college, I heard that stockbrokers make a lot of money. I looked up some brokers who were alumni, called one, and asked if I could meet him. I wanted to ask questions about his job and see firsthand what he did at work.

The broker's office was in Phoenix, Arizona. He got up early when trading opened in New York. I met him in the late afternoon. The first thing I noticed was he had to be there, glued to his computer and phone, available to his clients during trading hours. I couldn't see that working for me.

"Do you like your job?" I asked him.

"I like the money," he replied.

I understood. I thanked him and left. For me, no amount of money was worth being chained to an office. My goal of climbing mountains required flexibility and freedom.

Because You Can

Do What You Like

In climbing your mountain, you may find yourself scared of taking risks, scared of failure, or afraid of rejection. What gets me over my fear is passion. Even when it's stressful, I enjoy climbing.

In business, it helps if you enjoy your product and the service you are offering. It helps if it's more than just a paycheck. If you are in sales, you might love the thrill of the chase, developing strategy, the roller coaster ride, heartache, triumph, and agony of defeat. You might enjoy it because it's never boring.

If you are unsure what your passion or preference is, pretend you are dead. Imagine that you're lying on your deathbed, reflecting on your life. What would you have wanted to do to feel that you had lived a fulfilling life with no regrets? Each of us has an ambition in our closet, something we dreamed of doing but put on hold and buried deep inside us. Sometimes it rears its pesky head, and you think you should try it but can't imagine how to get started. It's a secret only you know, one you won't share with others for fear they may tell you it's too late, you're too old, not talented, or don't have enough money. It's a mountain that's never been climbed and a mountain you continue to dream of. Don't be afraid. Follow your dream and go big. You are the most powerful when you are authentic.

If you're not sure if something is your passion, think

Do What Interests You

romance. Are you in love with it? Passion is an emotion, an intense feeling of enthusiasm. It is boundless, sometimes dangerous, and makes you forget about everything else.

In *The Science of Getting Rich* (Wallace D. Wattles, 1910), the author writes:

> You can get rich in ANY business, for if you have not the right talent for it you can develop that talent; It will be EASIER for you to succeed in a vocation for which you already have talents in a well-developed state; but you CAN succeed in any vocation, for you can develop rudimentary talent. You will get rich in point of effort if you do that for which you are best fitted; but you will get rich most satisfactory if you do that which you WANT to do. Doing what you WANT to do is life; and there is no real satisfaction in living if we are compelled to be forever doing something which we do not like to do, and can never do what we want to do.

Finding Success in a J.O.B. Description

Thinking about what you would regret if you were dead may have gotten you motivated to take action. Pursuing your dream in life should be a goal. Not everyone, however, can or should immediately quit an unfulfilling job.

Because You Can

In the meantime, be successful where you are. Look at your job description and figure out how to excel within that boundary. Find what you're good at in the description and what you have a passion for.

A fact of life is that no one does everything in a job description. Different people come into the role. Some do certain things in a job description really well and don't do the other things quite as well because that's not what they are good at. Almost everyone, if they are competent, can do most things in a job description fairly well. You can, therefore, do everything and be mediocre. Or you can do most of the things and do some of them exceedingly well and excel.

What do You Desire?

Choose what you want and the how will fall into place.

The secret to happiness is astonishingly simple, though not necessarily easy to carry out: don't waste any more time on things that make you unhappy. Always be looking for options. Never stay longer than absolutely necessary in an unpleasant circumstance.

The purpose of the following exercise is to make sure the outcome you desire, your success, is what you truly desire. It can be surprisingly simple to achieve a goal when we are clear about what we want. Let go of needing to get *that* job, take *that* class, or date *that* person,

Do What Interests You

and ask yourself what you would enjoy. It might that the obstacle stopping you is having time. Make your goal finding time. Be specific. For example, "My goal is to have four hours a week to write a novel that's in my head." If you are in a dire circumstance, do not set the goal to get out. Exceed that by imagining things better than they were before.

If you are not sure of what you want, consider the following:

What will not happen when you get it?
What will happen if you don't get it?
How will you get it?
What's stopping you?

After considering these questions, if your goal is still one you want to pursue, then continue. If you are not clear about what you want, or can't commit to what is required to be successful, don't start. You're wasting time. Most of those who fail do so because they don't have a clear vision of what they want before they get started.

The Nose

The Nose on El Capitan in Yosemite was my first big rock climb. Most climbers don't choose the biggest rock climb in the world to be their first big climb. I fell in love

Because You Can

with the mountain when I was a teenager and saw a picture of it in *Yosemite Climber*. It is what inspired me to learn to rock climb. My heart wasn't into climbing smaller mountains first. I would rather have failed on the Nose than try to climb something else first. It's what I had a passion for.

At the time, I was working full time and going to college. Scheduling a week off from work and school at the same time was difficult. There was a narrow window in which I could try to climb it before summer school started. I took a week of vacation, all that I had, and drove to Yosemite by myself.

At the campgrounds, I found a note on the bulletin board from a man from Australia who was looking for

Do What Interests You

partners. He had already hooked up with a Canadian but invited me to join them. I was delighted. I explained I didn't have as much experience as they did. I promised to be the engine that could.

On the first day, we fixed ropes up to Sickle ledge, a big ledge 600 feet off the ground, and came down for the night. I thought things were going well. (To "fix" a rope means to tie the end to an anchor and leave the ropes hanging so you can use it to pull yourself up when you return.)

The next day we returned, hauled our bag with food and water up there, and slept on the ledge. The following morning we started climbing higher, with hopes of reaching the next ledge big enough for us to sleep on before it got dark. Almost a thousand of feet of difficult climbing separated us from it.

We were still several hundred feet from our sleeping spot when it was my turn to lead. I moved slow, afraid I might fall. The sun was starting to go down. I saw where I needed to go, but I was scared. As I craned my head and looked above, I saw a wall of steep, smooth granite as far as I could see. I yelled down to my partners that I was stuck.

My partners were around the corner, unable to see me. After desperately trying to communicate through the wind, I heard them yell that if I had enough gear, I should set up an anchor where I was. It was not the normal stopping place. Clanking in the wind at my feet was a "No

Because You Can

Parking" sign. Some jokester had bolted it to the rock there. I was the most terrified I had ever been.

When my partners reached me, useless arguments ensued. The immediate question was where to sleep. The sun was going down. I give the Aussie credit for everything that happened next. He spotted a small, sloping ledge that was twenty feet down, large enough for the three of us to sit on. We lowered ourselves — just us, not our sleeping bags. We slept side by side, sitting with our feet dangling over the ledge, the rope tethering us to the anchor twenty feet above.

In the morning, the question of if we should continue or go down was discussed. I sat quietly as to let the others make the decision. I had pooped in my pants and a loaf was stuck. I was miserable and voted in my head to bail. But I didn't want to ruin it for them.

The Aussie and Canadian, no poop in their pants, no school or jobs to go to, voted to go down.

We had swung around a corner. Below us was a blank face for 1,000 feet. Complicating the nature of retreat was that we had to go down with a haul bag containing three people's sleeping gear and food. I'm grateful for the guidance and expertise of the Aussie. While this might seem more of a survival story than a feeling of triumph and satisfaction of doing what interests you, I was happy. I learned from the experience and planned to go back. I was still passionate about climbing, about *being* on the Nose. This wasn't about conquering a hard

Do What Interests You

The five-gallon drum of water we put in our haul bag.

thing. I simply had a desire to be there.

The following year, I wanted to go back and try again. I was worried I might still be too slow. I told a friend about my doubts. He had climbed the Nose, and I expected him to concur, to tell me that I was not ready. Instead of agreeing with my insecurities, however, he encouraged me. He said if I had enough time and desire, I could get up anything. He said to bring plenty of water (gallons more than you think you need), take your time (we took a week of food), and if you are slow, let others pass.

I drove to Yosemite where I met Derrick, a partner, by placing a note on the bulletin board in the campground. I brought the largest Army Surplus duffle bag sold and wrapped duck-tape around it to prevent it from being

Because You Can

The Army duffle bag protected with duck tape, being dragged up the mountain. It contained five gallons of water and food for a week.

torn as we dragged it up the mountain behind us. The first item we placed inside was the drum of water. We wrapped our sleeping bags around it to protect it.

It was Derrick's turn to go first when we reached the part that had scared me the year before. When he was high up and around the corner, in a place I could not see him, he quit moving. I held the rope, as though waiting for a fish to bite; ready to hold the rope tight if he fell. Finally, word came. He was stuck. I knew exactly what to do. He was at the No Parking sign. I told him to set an anchor, and I would come up. I wasn't afraid. I'd been practicing for this day.

The crack was the same width for as far as the eye could see. We had only three pieces of gear that would fit. To climb it, I did what's called "leap-frogging." I put a piece of gear in the crack and stood on it. Then I reached above my head and placed another. I pulled up

Do What Interests You

and stood on it, then reached down and removed the one I had been standing on. I repeated this until I made it to the anchor, which was 150 feet above us. After that, the rest of the climb seemed easy. Realizing I had skills, I became confident in my abilities. Like a Jedi master, I had become fearless.

Boot Flake on El Capitan

Main Takeaway

Tap into your passion and harness that — it will grow your power and your impact.

Be Where You Are

All journeys have secret destinations of which the traveler is unaware.
- Martin Buber

I have a friend whose primary residence is in Las Vegas, Nevada. He spends summers renting a house in Santa Barbara, visits his dad in Florida for a month in the fall, and then goes to Costa Rica in the winter. As he was getting ready to return to Las Vegas after being gone for months, I asked him, "Aren't you glad you're going home?"

"Home is here," he replied. He was still in Costa Rica.

"Yes, but you own a condo in Las Vegas. That's where the post office sends your mail. Isn't that your home?"

"Home is where I am."

Wherever you are, be there. Immerse yourself. Stay present. If you're not in the moment, you can hurt yourself or lose the game. When I'm on a mountain, in a difficult and uncomfortable situation, the kind I wish I could be anywhere else, ones I wish a helicopter could whisk me away from, I recall my motto: "I am where I am." I don't allow myself be distracted by thoughts about what I am going to do later. To be successful, to keep myself and partners from getting hurt or killed, I have to stay focused. I have no choice. It has to be. Mistakes happen when you lose concentration and don't stay focused on the task at hand

To stay focused in the present moment doesn't mean you should not take the time to smell the roses. I'm always looking around at the scenery — it's one of the reasons I climb. To stay present means your thoughts are about the scene. If you play sports, it might be appreciating the fans or noticing a player's form that helps you stay focused. By doing so you are more likely to achieve your desired outcome — winning the game.

In the following story, when I smelled rain and snow from an impending storm. My thoughts shifted from how pretty the dark clouds were to what was required to safely climb through the storm. I didn't let my mind drift into thinking about how nice it would be to sleep in my own bed.

The Zodiac

Every climber dreams of climbing the Zodiac, a climb on El Capitan in Yosemite. I fell in love with it while reading climbing books and seeing photos of climbers hanging on the side of the mountain. Since I was short

Be Where You Are

on time off from work, my friend and climbing partner, Vince, went to Yosemite a few days before I got there and started climbing the route. He climbed the first two pitches (rope lengths) and came down to wait for me. He left the ropes hanging so that we could use them to get back up to his high point.

    I didn't know how I'd find enough time to meet Vince.

Because You Can

Be Where You Are

Staying in the moment, I went into the office at the corporation I worked at and made an appearance. Then, at 10:30 a.m., I left for an early lunch. My expectation was that when others didn't see me at my desk, they would think I was in one of the many daily meetings professionals in big corporations spend their time. I went home, got my climbing gear, and drove across the street to get food for the trip. It was Thursday morning. The grocery store was on the corner by my house. As I was leaving the store, I was surprised by who I saw - my older brother, John, who just so happened to work at the same company.

"John!" I said with a big smile, "what are you doing here?"

"Getting lunch."

"Really?" I said, amazed at the coincidence. I went to the store several times a week and had never seen him there before.

"What are *you* up to?" he asked.

""Just getting a little snack." I presented a bagel and yogurt as evidence and feigned innocence. I didn't want to chat for too long. I thought if I told my brother I was going climbing, he'd lecture me, big brother style, on how it was wrong to be skipping out of work to climb.

"See you later," I said.

I rushed out the door, got in my truck, and started driving to Yosemite. I drove through the night and arrived at Camp 4, the unofficial climber's camp, at 11

Because You Can

p.m. Vince had reserved a campground for us and was waiting there for me.

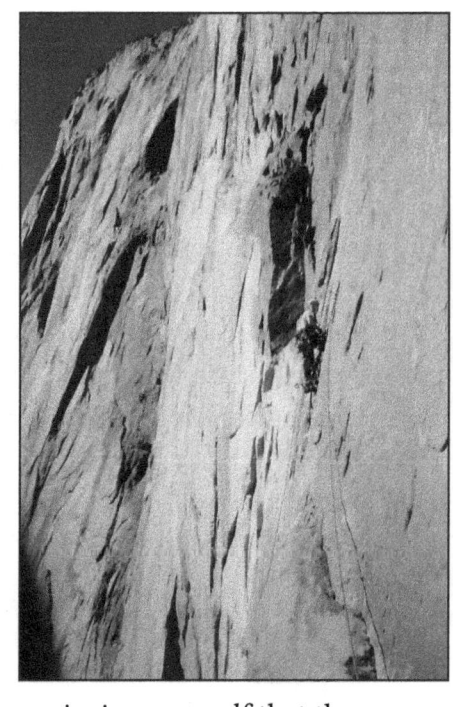

The Zodiac is sixteen pitches, or sixteen rope lengths, long. Vince had fixed two ropes (left two ropes hanging on the mountain for us to go up). That left fourteen to go. We estimated we could climb three to four each day. Every climber will tell you they think they can climb farther each day than they actually can. It's wishful thinking, a way of convincing yourself that the mountain you want to climb is not as big as it actually is.

As I tried to stay in the present moment, I became concerned about what would happen if we were slower than expected and I was late getting back to work. My logic was that if I drove back on Monday, I could be back in the office the same day.

I chose to stop worrying, to stop thinking about it, and to focus on climbing. With so little time to spare, we should have started climbing immediately. Vince, however, saw that I was tired from driving and in no

Be Where You Are

shape to safely jump on a wall (a big mountain). Instead, we decided to take it easy for a day. We visited the places tourists go, the ones climbers never take time to see. We got burgers and had ice cream, put our feet in the Merced River, and sat in El Cap Meadows. We got a good night's sleep, and in the morning, I was rested and ready to go.

On Saturday, we hung in our ledges on the side of the mountain at the top of pitch 6. On Sunday, we reached the top of pitch 8. Going two pitches a day put us far behind schedule for me to get back to work on time. And as we reached pitch 14, the weather changed.

Because You Can

Yosemite is in the High Sierra. Although it is only hours inland by car, it's close enough to the ocean to bring sufficient amounts of moisture that can turn warm rain into freezing rain and snow. Climbers have perished in Yosemite, when the weather has changed from hot and sunny to cold rain and snow. This is when I really had to focus, to forget about how late I was going to be getting back to work, and stay in the moment.

Two days later we reached the top. It took us five

Be Where You Are

hours to get down. At 9 p.m. we were drinking Bailey's and coffee in the Mountain Room Bar. It was a tradition to go there after a big climb. Cold and wet, I made sure to only have only one glass. I was enjoying a moment I knew couldn't last.

At 11 p.m., I got into my truck, parked frozen on the side of the road at the bottom of the mountain, and began driving home. It was Thursday night. A week had gone by. I didn't have a cell phone and didn't bother to stop and look for a pay phone. I made it to Los Angeles before pulling over, exhausted as it became daylight, stuck in morning traffic. I thought it better use of time to take a nap and return to driving after rush hour (if there's such a thing as less traffic in L.A.)

I got off the freeway and found a pay phone where I could nap inside my car. Not having change made it difficult. I eventually reached the operator at the company I worked for and was connected to the secretary in my office. I got the answering machine. After a two-hour nap, I finished driving home.

The first thing I did when I got home was check my message machine. The machine was full. I played the first one.

"Hey, this is your brother, John. Nobody has seen you in a while. We're worried. Call me."

The next was: "Dan, this is Mike from work. I haven't seen you at work in a few days. John says you don't return any of his calls."

Because You Can

The next was: "Daniel, this is your mother. No one has seen you in days. I'm worried."

I called my brother first. At work, he had run into Mike, my cubical mate. They had decided to ransack my office to look for clues as to my whereabouts, and then my apartment. My younger brother had suggested to them, "He's probably climbing. Call the national parks. Start with Yosemite." At first, they didn't. When they did, a ranger in Yosemite went to look and got back to them: "Yes, his truck is here. We had a big storm. We went out and asked, and they said they were OK."

As I went into work the next day, I prepared my mind to stay focused, calm, and not to worry. My strategy was to breathe and pretend that everything was OK. Let them come to you. Sit quietly at your desk. Act like you're doing something, but don't do anything that takes you away from being focused on being calm. If your cubical mate is at his desk, don't talk. Don't say anything more than what's required. The boss isn't going to talk to you in front of others. He's going to ask you to come into his office. When you return, fellow employees will ask what happened. Don't talk. Pretend you have somewhere to go, something to do.

I sat there, staring at the screen on the computer on my desk when I heard his voice.

"Dan, I'd like to see you in my office please." It was my boss, Tom.

Without a word, I got up, pushed my chair in, and

Be Where You Are

Because You Can

followed Tom into his office. He sat behind his desk. I stood in the doorway, afraid to move inside.

"Mick would like to see you in his office." Mick was Tom's boss. Mick's office was down the hall, where upper management was located.

"OK."

I left Tom's office, walked past rows of cubicles, and out the door into a big hallway. I walked to the end, where, through a small, nondescript door, the entry to the offices for upper management. They don't like to be bothered with small stuff.

Josie, the head secretary, was sitting behind her desk, just inside the door.

"Hi Josie," I said, faking a smile as if everything was OK. "I'm here to see Mick."

"Go right in. He's expecting you."

I walked past her desk and entered the inner sanctum, a corridor to the offices for upper managers. Mick's office was the first, the biggest. His door was open. I stood in the doorway and waited for him to notice me.

"Have a seat," he said with a big smile and half a grin.

I sat down in a comfortable, leather chair in front of his desk.

"What happened?" he asked me calmly.

I began to tell my story: "I was climbing... when a big storm came in..." I kept it short, taking my time, assessing his reactions to check if I should stick to my script or change course. "We didn't need to be rescued," I con-

Be Where You Are

tinued. "We kept moving, albeit slowly and carefully."

I paused and waited for a response as to how the boss felt. After a short moment of silence, with his trademark grin and half-smile, he said, "I just think you're crazy."

I waited for more as I wondered what my punishment might be. After a few more moments of silence, I got the feeling that was all he had to say. I decided to leave while things were good. I got up, motioned goodbye, and walked out of his office.

Being Where You Are

To be where you are means to have faith that everything is and will be OK. You will find a way. Whatever your predicament is, don't think, "I should have done this, could have done that, wish I had done that, or if only I had done that." Be gentle with yourself. You're doing better than you give yourself credit. Enjoy the place, the space, to get where you are going. Stay focused on the task at hand. Don't think about tomorrow. It will be here soon enough.

Takeaway

Being in the moment gives you power and strength.

Because You Can

Extract Yourself

When you're the best version of yourself, who are you? Where are you when you are the best version of yourself?

Sometimes you need to get away from it all — the people, the place, the circumstance you find yourself in. I call this an extraction. It might be you need to extract yourself from your environment. It might be you help a friend by removing him or her from a bad situation. In the following story, my nephew needed to be extracted from the city he lived in to prevent contact between him and gang members who were peer-pressuring him at high school.

The Blob

Our story begins as I was in bed getting ready to fall asleep and heard my phone ring. It was late, so I ignored it. It rang again.

I got out of bed and looked to see who called. It was my older brother, John. He was leaving town on a business trip in the morning and his wife had to work at a new job. He was calling for advice regarding his teenage son, Nate.

Nate was getting peer-pressure at high school from friends who were gang members. They wanted him to hang out with them. Nate could tell trouble was brewing and worried that after his parents left in the morning, gang members were going to come and get him and they might do something stupid.

I wasn't sure what to tell my brother. I hung up the phone and checked the time. It was an eight-hour drive from my house to their home in Phoenix, Arizona. I calculated if I left immediately, I could make it to their house by morning, in time to keep an eye on Nate after his parents left.

I got in my Jeep, drove through the night, and arrived at their home at 8 a.m. Nate was in bed, sleeping.

"Nate," I said, "It's uncle Dan. I need your help. Can you come with me back to my house and help me with work? I'll pay you."

Nate was into making money and agreed to go with me. We drove back to my house in New Mexico. I had told Nate about making money. I had not told him about climbing. After a week of working, I broke the news to him that we needed to go climbing. I wanted to return to an area of Zion Nation Park where a group of mountains called the Bishoprics are located. A month earlier I had tried to climb the North Bishopric, a mountain that

Extract Yourself

had not been climbed before. An obstacle called the Blob was in the way. Getting past it looked uncertain. Like myself, other climbers had attempted and failed to get to the top of the North Bishopric. I wanted to return to investigate the Blob before it got cold and started to snow. It was already mid-November.

Only seventeen, Nate had never climbed or rappelled. In fact, he'd never been on a long hike and didn't own a pair of hiking boots. I dug through my closet to outfit him with the basic gear he needed: harness, helmet, and rappel device (for going down a rope). I dug out a rain jacket, down jacket (it would be cold), headlamp, sleeping bag, and so forth. I piled everything in a big heap on my living room floor. I didn't have climbing shoes that fit him, so he wore his Timberland (a brand of fancy, leather, street boots). He wore jeans and a Bern bicycling helmet. I told him to take whatever he wanted. It wasn't on the pile. He saw it in the corner in my living room — my Charlet Mosser ice axe. He thought it might be useful to climb steep rock. I didn't tell him that rock climbers don't use ice axes.

The plan was to try and

Because You Can

climb what I and other good climbers had previously never attempted to scale: the Blob. This might sound ridiculous considering better climbers had assumed it too difficult. But those climbers, including myself, had never tried. We had looked at the Blob from a distance and concluded that even if one climbed it, it would be impossible to get to the top of the North Bishopric from the other side. But none of us had stood on top of the Blob, gone down the other side, and verified that. To me, it seemed the worst thing that could happen to Nate and I is that once we got there, we would find it to be too difficult and come down. Since reaching the Blob involved only a lot of hiking, camping, and easier climbing, I felt it was an outing I could safely take Nate.

Extract Yourself

We started hiking in the late afternoon. At 10 p.m., Nate told me he thought a mountain lion was following us. In the dark he saw the red eyes of deer. Deer seemed to be following us. Then he thought there might be bears following. I explained that animals are normally more scared of us than we are of them. I didn't tell him that near our camp the following night, we would be close to Cougar Mountain, named so because of the large number of mountain lions.

We camped near the edge of a cliff overlooking a valley. In the morning, we rappelled down the cliff using 400 feet of rope. We left the ropes hanging so that we could use them get back up when we were finished. The mountain, the Blob, was on the other side of the valley. From there on, there were no trails to get to where we

Because You Can

were going. I explained that the easiest way could be found following deer trails and droppings. Nate became an excellent deer trail finder.

The next day, I taught Nate the basics of how to hold the rope in case I fell. I tied one end of the rope to a tree and had Nate clip himself to the tree. Safely tied to the tree, he fed rope out to me as I climbed. When I got to the end of the rope, I set up an anchor, and he climbed up to meet me. We repeated the process as we made our way to the top of the Gatekeeper, the first peak on our way to the Blob. We went down the other side and kept going. We were on virgin, unexplored territory. The Blob rose up from the ridge like a big obstacle between

Extract Yourself

us and the North Bishopric.

With Nate's presence, I found the Blob to be easy to climb. When I reached the top, I sat down, tied myself to a large rock, and told Nate to start climbing as I pulled up the slack in the rope between us. We had made it past the Blob and to the bottom of the North Bishopric, a place no one had ever been.

I wanted to try and climb the North Bishopric, but it was late in the afternoon, and we may have run out of daylight. We looked for a way to get down. We could not go back the way we had come. We wrapped the rope around a tree on the edge and threw both ends down the west face of the ridge we were on. After we went down

the ropes and were safe at another tree, we pulled the ropes down to use them again. We repeated this past six trees, naming it Nate's Tree Descent. We spent the night in camp.

The hardest part was getting out, back up the ropes we left hanging, to get back to the trail in the high country. To go up the ropes, we had jumars (known as ascenders). A jumar is a device that clamps onto a rope and will slide up but not down it. It's strenuous to pull yourself up a rope using jumars, awkward, and, when hanging on the rope, terrifying.

There were two ropes to go up. I had Nate go first. I explained what to do. Once he was off the ground, there was nothing I could do but shout encouragements. At first he moved fast. Then, as he got tired and the rock became steeper, he slowed to a crawl. Occasionally he yelled down for advice. There was none I could give. Then, the unexpected came. In the proudest voice he yelled down, "Uncle Dan! I'm at the top!"

The second rope was shorter but more challenging to ascend. The top edge of the cliff stuck out. The rope hung over a lip at the top, like that of a coffee pot spout. With weight on the rope, the rope wanted to lay flat on the spout. Ten feet from the top, Nate couldn't slide his jumars up the rope. He gave it his best effort. Hanging in the air, exhausted, in a soft, defeated voice he announced, "Uncle Dan... I can't do it."

While Nate had been struggling, I had been thinking.

Extract Yourself

I knew the rope was going over the edge of the spout. When planning our trip, I had special ordered an extremely thick rope to put there. It was 11.4 millimeters in diameter and a *static* rope, meaning no matter how hard you bounced on it, it wouldn't stretch. No matter how much Nate and I bounced on it, it wouldn't wear through. It was marketed as assault line.

I did what might never cross the mind of a normal climber. With Nate still hanging on the rope, I got on the rope and went up behind him. The rope was strong enough to hold both of us and our bags of gear. I went up the rope until my head was at Nate's feet.

"Have you done this before?" Nate asked in a calm, doubting voice.

I had, and I could tell Nate endless stories and what I had learned from them. We'd find a way. We'd just begun.

I tried to give Nate a boost and push him to the top. When that didn't work, I told him to stand on my shoulders. That didn't work.

"Have you done this before?" Nate asked again, in a calm and concerned voice.

I laughed. I didn't answer. My mind was occupied. I was scanning the face of the rock, waiting for another idea. It may have been obvious to you before it was to me — with both Nate and my weight on the rope, it was even more difficult for Nate to slide his jumars up. Then I got an idea.

Because You Can

There were footholds on the rock face to the side of Nate. I found some handholds and free-climbed past him. As I worked around him, I grabbed the rope above him and pulled myself to the top. I reached my hand down to Nate to take his weight off the rope, and he slid his ascender up it. We made it to the top.

We finished hiking in the dark and reached my Jeep at 10 p.m. I don't carry a phone in the backcountry. On the way to Las Vegas I checked my messages. Nate had missed an appointment with the principal at his high

Extract Yourself

school, where he had been a no-show. His location and date of return were unknown to them. It didn't go over well with the school board when his dad told them Nate was in the wilderness climbing with his uncle. But they understood the confidential nature of an extraction. For an extraction to be effective, only those with a need to know should know the details.

While we were climbing, the gang members who had been peer-pressuring Nate were arrested for burglary. Their pictures were in the newspaper. He never saw them again. He caught up in school, and at the end of the semester, he graduated from high school at the top of his class. Today, when I stop by, he's quick to let me know he has a college class to go to. I can't blame him for not wanting go climbing again. He probably thinks that's how climbing is supposed to be: a long and epic adventure. I returned the following spring and climbed to the top of the North Bishopric.

Transforming Uncertainty into Taking Action

Make a list of your friends. Circle the ones you enjoy spending time with. Cross-out those you do not. Cross out those who do not bring out the best in you, along with those who do not make you a better person. Choose to associate only with those who bring out the best in you. Leave space at the bottom to add new ones. Make a list and do the same with professionals at work and in your occupation.

This advice will help when we get to How to Make No-lose Decisions in the chapter titled Take Risks. If you're careful to associate only with those who offer you positive and helpful criticism, you will have a circle of people from which you can seek clear and helpful advice. They will be friends and colleagues you can trust, those who want to see you succeed.

Main Takeaway

Sometimes the best way to move forward is to get out of the place/situation/relationship you're in.

Discover the Truth

All truths are easy to understand once they are discovered. The point is to discover them.
- Galileo Galilei

Some think Edison invented the light bulb. In fact, light bulbs had been invented before Edison was born. The bulbs burnt out in few hours, making them unsuitable for homes. Edison realized the problem was the filament, and he tried thousands of alternative materials for filaments before he found one that lasted. Henceforth, he formed a partnership with his competitor, and Edison-Swan United became the world's largest manufacturer of light bulbs.

People ask how I know if a mountain has been climbed. It's a good question. There are no record books. I study history books and visit park rangers. I climb mountains that have been climbed and are in guidebooks and look around when I'm at the top. When possible, I ask climbers who live near a climb. But explorers tend to guard their plans carefully, making it difficult to get straight answers.

Because You Can

If you want to understand what's going on in this rapidly changing world, approach the media with a critical eye. Learn how to separate fact from fiction. Doctored videos, propaganda, and speculation reported as fact, compounded by people copying and proliferating misinformation, can make it difficult to discern the truth. Rarely does a story tell the whole story. Consider the sources, ask questions, and go deep.

The First Modern Climbing Fatality in Zion National Park — The Rest of the Story

A few days before New Year's Eve, 1996, I drove to Zion to meet my friend, Vince. We were planning on climbing the Lowe Route, the longest route on the mountain called Angels Landing in Zion National Park. I arrived a day early to fix rope at the start of the climb. Vince was bringing a friend from Russia, so I got a permit for three people. I parked in the empty parking lot in front of the mountain and began sorting the gear I would need. As I was packing, another climber parked next to me.

Bob was by himself and asked what I was up to. I explained I would be fixing rope to a big ledge on the mountain, and when my friends arrived, we would finish climbing to the top. Bob asked if he could join me. He understood that when my friends arrived he might not be able to finish the climb with us. He said he would rather get some climbing done than none, and I liked

Discover the Truth

the idea of having a partner. We became friends and climbed to the top of the big ledge together. When we got to the ledge, we tied the ropes together and rappelled to the ground. As we reached the ground, Vince and Vladimir arrived.

Vince and Vladimir were OK with Bob joining the team. The next day, we crossed the river with food, sleeping bags, portaledges, and all the necessities to climb a big wall in the winter. It was foggy and overcast. Rain and snow were in the forecast.

On our third day of climbing, we noticed someone climbing Prodigal Sun, a route to the right of us. Prodigal Sun is shorter and easier, a route many climbers do their first time in Zion. Vince and I had climbed Prodigal Sun on our first trip to Zion in 1991. We took our time and slept on the side of the mountain — twice. On the second night we were close to the top but didn't make it. We stopped at a ledge called the Emergency Bivy. It was Vince's idea. He was always the smart one. Maybe that's why he made such a good pilot. In the morning, when we were able to see where we were going, we scrambled sideways to the trail and walked down the backside of the mountain to the parking lot.

The climber we saw was John Christensen. I took pictures of him as he climbed. I thought it would be nice to give them to him when he got down. His van was parked next to my truck.

John fixed two ropes that day, came down, and then

Because You Can

Although technically one of the easier climbing routes, Prodigal Sun is steep! Opposite page: John Christensen (circled), soloing Prodigal Sun.

went to his van to sleep. He was planning on finishing the climb the next day, New Year's Eve. By fixing the two ropes, he had given himself a head start.

The next day, John hauled himself up his fixed ropes and proceeded to finish the climb. Late in the afternoon he slowed down. It's hard work climbing by yourself. After you climb up as far as the rope will reach, you secure it to an anchor, rappel down, untie the rope from the bottom anchor, and use the rope to hoist yourself back up. You hence climb the mountain twice.

Because You Can

The last picture I took of John was in the late afternoon of December 31st. He was high on the wall, looking confident and secure. At 9 p.m., as he used his headlamp to continue, I got into my sleeping bag and pulled the top over my head. It was cold.

In the morning there was no sight of John. I assumed he had finished the climb and hiked the trail down the backside of the mountain. Vince suspected otherwise.

"Did you hear that scream in the middle of the night?" he suggested. "I'll bet you that was that climber on Prodigal Sun."

I shrugged his comment off. I didn't hear a scream and couldn't imagine that what he had heard was a climber falling to his death.

That same day, John's wife called the park service and reported him overdue. Rangers drove to the parking lot at Angels Landing and looked for him climbing. They didn't see him. They saw Bob, Vince, Vladimir, and myself. The river was flowing fast. They didn't want to cross it to look for John at the bottom of the climb. When they didn't see a climber on Prodigal Sun, they thought John might be climbing with us. My permit was for three people. I hadn't added Bob. The park rangers called John's wife and told her that they thought John might be climbing with us.

Two things should have raised doubts about the possibility that John could be climbing with us. When John started climbing, we were already halfway up the moun-

Discover the Truth

tain. Our ropes could not have reached the ground for him to join us. His wife protested her disagreement with their idea. If John was going to climb a different and more difficult route, and climb it with strangers for several days, he would have told her.

We reached to the top that evening, soaked in the rain. After hauling our gear to the top, we walked down the trail and went to the campgrounds for the night.

In the morning, I was woken by a tap-tap-tap on the window of my pickup. I was sleeping, curled in the front seat. My truck didn't have a shell, and it was raining, the ground soggy with puddles. I didn't have a tent. In my slumber, my first thought was that I was in trouble for not paying the camping fee. Then I remembered that my friends had paid it. I rolled the window down.

"Hi," the ranger said through the gap at the top of the window as he stood in the rain. "We're looking for a John Christensen, a climber that was supposed to be climbing Prodigal Sun. We thought he might be climbing with you guys."

I thought for a minute, half-asleep, still surprised I wasn't in trouble for something.

"No," I replied, "I don't know him. He's not with us."

"Don't leave," the ranger instructed. "A special investigator is on the way. She'd like to speak with you."

I didn't understand what was happening. I got out of my truck, skipped across puddles of mud to Vince's van, and knocked on its back door. Vince knew exactly what was happening.

"You know who they're looking for," he said with the confidence of a pilot hitting turbulence, "that guy that was climbing Prodigal Sun."

At that point, the park service initiated a Search and Rescue (SAR) to look for John. They decided it was too dangerous to cross the river as we had done to get to the bottom of the climb. The team instead crossed a footbridge some distance down the river and hiked back along on other side, where they found John's body at the bottom. It was January 2nd.

The story run by the Associated Press was that a climber died when a botched rappel caused him to fall to his death. The news said there were no witnesses, and he got to the top but decided to rappel instead of walking the trail down. Rangers speculated that rock fall might have been a factor. Based on press reports, the author of *Deaths in Zion National Park* wrote, "It took searchers only a short time to find his body at the base of the peak."

The SAR team reported that the cause of death was likely the climber had used ropes of different thickness causing the ropes to slip as he was rappelling. Readers were left to think that John was either too lazy to walk down from the top using the trail or didn't realize how ropes of different thickness may behave when you rappel on them. Neither of these are true. John did not make it to the top, and the thickness of his ropes was

Discover the Truth

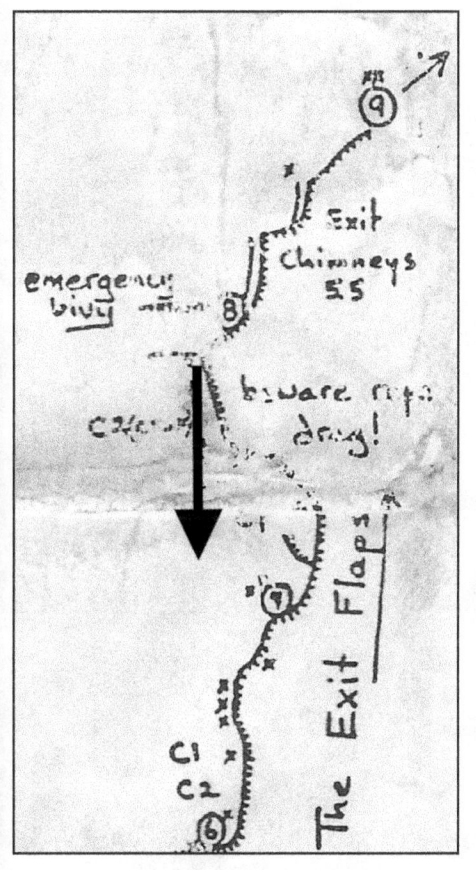

Excerpt from the map climbers use. The arrow indicates the direction John was coming down. Near the tip of the arrow he needed to go sideways to reach the spot marked "7", the 7th anchor. Instead, he kept going straight down, and in the dark, he didn't realize that he had come to the end of his rope.

not a factor in his death.

John did not make it to the top. He reached the emergency bivy, a flat spot 100 feet from the top. You don't want to stop there, but if it's dark, you are grateful for the opportunity to have a flat ledge to sleep on. The climb at that point does not go up. It goes sideways and looks impossible in the dark. If you get there in the dark, you are confused and find yourself stuck and unsure of how to continue. You sleep on the ledge and wait for morning.

Judging from where I took my last pictures of him, John likely reached to the emergency bivy early in the night. He may have waited some time before he decided

Angel's Landing. On the left is the Lowe Route that we were climbing. On the right is Prodigal Sun, the route John Christensen was climbing. Circled and sideways, which here is shown under the emergency bivy, is the anchor John needed to swing to as he was rappelling from the Emergency Bivy.

Discover the Truth

to go down. He must have been very cold without camping gear. After midnight, he probably decided to go down by rappelling, most likely because he was freezing to death. I suspect he took a calculated risk. The longer he stayed on the ledge, the colder he would become. He decided to go down while he still had the mental and physical capacity that rappelling the ropes required.

To rappel a cliff taller than the length of your rope, you must stop on the way down at the same anchors you stopped at when you climbed up it. At each anchor, you pull the ropes and use them to go down to the next anchor. The process is repeated until you reach the ground.

Now consider what doing this would be like in the dark when you can't see the anchors below you until you are nearly at them. You can only see so far with a headlamp, and this was before the bright LED headlamps that are available today. In addition, the metal bolts used for the anchors are painted red to be camouflaged so they are not an eyesore to tourists in the daytime.

In the pitch black, John could not see the end of his rope as he searched for the next anchor. He didn't see the anchor because it was not below him: it was several feet to the side.

The route between the emergency bivy and the anchor below is diagonal. He would have had to swing over to the anchor. John was looking down, when he passed the anchor and ran out of rope. It was then he went off the

Because You Can

end of his ropes. The accident had nothing to do with equipment error or being too lazy to walk the trail down from the top.

The Associated Press said that coverage was limited to the statements made by investigator Dave Bucchello. Bucchello was not the investigator who spoke to us. The special investigator sent to question me and my climbing partners was a woman, someone without climbing experience, one without knowledge of the climbing routes.

I told her I had taken pictures of John and wanted his family to have them. I said I would mail her a set of prints and the negatives after I got the film developed. As we talked, the rain turned to snow. Puddles turned to ice. I called Ron, my normal climbing partner, to see if he wanted to meet me in Zion. We had tentative plans to climb something else.

"There's a big storm coming your way," he warned. "There's no way you're going to avoid it. Get out now."

It seemed I needed to start driving home before treacherous weather made it dangerous in my two-wheel drive, so I left the park and drove home.

When I developed the film, I was surprised at how clear the images of John are considering the pictures were taken using a disposable camera in a cardboard box with a fixed lens. The park service would not release his family's contact information, so I sent a copy of the prints and negatives to the special investigator.

Discover the Truth

Exactly one year later, I received a call from John's wife. The park service had finally given her my contact information. She said the park service told her they lost the negatives. She was upset because his death certificate says January 2nd. Death certificates are dated at the time a body is recovered. She thought there must be more to the official story and asked me for clarity. I told her what I knew.

Rest in peace, John.

Transforming Uncertainty into Taking Action

How do you know?

When you hear a story about someone's failure, it can be helpful to unpack it and question whether that is truly what happened or if there were other obstacles you are not hearing about, ones you need to know so that you can overcome them.

Main Takeaway

Question everything. Sometimes what you read in a newspaper, online, or discover in a book is not accurate or true.

Some have suggested John was unprepared and selfish. The route is one of the easiest, and he had given himself a headstart. The fact that the news got the story wrong shows that none could have predicted what happened.

Because You Can

Luck Favors the Prepared

Chance (fortune) favors the prepared mind.
- Louis Pasteur

In business, they say you must plan, then execute, break it down, and plan for contingencies. If you don't have a well thoughtout plan, why are you doing it? Planning might involve stating the goal (what you really want), determining the resources that are required (what's crucial, and if we really need all that other stuff), understanding the risks, and being OK with the commitment required. It may mean coming together as a team and developing a leadership.

I do a lot of planning before a big climb. However, I believe preparing the mind is the most important element. You'll never be fully ready and perfect. To prepare for success just means being the person you need to be to take action and not hesitating when opportunities present themselves.

Because You Can

Light is Right

Our goal was to climb Mt. Sneffels in Colorado and to do so in the winter. On the drive there, we stopped in Telluride to buy sleds to haul our gear behind us. It's what is typically done to climb a big mountain such as those in Alaska.

The store didn't have what we were looking for. We settled for blow-up rafts, the type used in swimming pools, and rigged a method of pulling the rafts behind us with rope. We didn't have cross-country skis or the type of bindings that allow heels to pivot. We rented normal skis without skins. The skis did not have the parts that provide traction for going uphill. This wasn't because we weren't prepared: we didn't have the money to buy fancy gear. So we improvised. If we had been able to acquire better gear, we would have missed an opportunity to discover a strategy that would ultimately lead to our success on many other difficult climbs.

Luck Favors the Prepared

As we approached the mountain, I kept sliding backwards on my skis, and the rafts kept tipping over. It was frustrating and slow. At the end of the day, as we were setting up the tent, Ron realized he had forgotten matches. (OK — that was either not being prepared or a stroke of good fortune yet to be realized.) We needed to melt snow to have water to drink, so we skied back to the truck.

We took a break and discussed strategy, brainstorming what we could do to lighten our loads and move faster. The first idea was to ditch the tent. Next to go were our sleeping bags. Although it was winter in Colorado, we decided we could sleep in our cloths.

It was snowing with zero visibility. Based on compass readings, we proceeded in the direction of the mountain. As it got dark, we found a place under the trees with less snow on the ground, laid down, and went to sleep.

I woke in the middle of the night and had trouble feeling my toes. I was cold everywhere and shivering. We got up, gathered pieces of wet wood, and used gas from the stove to start a fire. Saved!

We were unsuccessful in climbing that mountain, but we learned what conditions we could survive without sleeping bags. We realized if we were willing to suffer being cold, we could climb bigger mountains faster, without carrying as much gear. We were better prepared for the next time.

Because You Can

Our experiment to climb without sleeping bags came in handy when we climbed the Matterhorn in Switzerland. On the way down from the top, we got lost in the dark. We reached a spot where I was unsure which way to go. It seemed there was a cliff ahead if we continued straight down.

I decided to go sideways and came to a rock face. Looking for handholds with my headlamp, I climbed to the top of the rock outcropping, looked down the other side, and saw a swath of steep, blue ice reflecting in the moonlight. A cold wind blew across my face. *Can't go down there*, I thought.

I took a glove off and stuck a finger in the air like one might to do to check which way the wind is blowing. Exposing my fingers to the cold wind, I knew we could survive. We had a choice — continue going down the mountain at great risk or sleep on it: literally.

Zermatt, the village at the bottom of the Matterhorn, is famous for its graveyard. It is filled with those who died while climbing the Matterhorn. I listened to my inner voice. *Stay put. You will live.*

Satisfied, I climbed down to Ronnie and told him the news: "We're stuck. There's no way that I can find."

Ron concurred. We began to clear a spot to sleep. We kicked with our boots to move rocks and flatten a spot, creating a small ledge on the side of the mountain on

Luck Favors the Prepared

which to sit, piling bigger rocks on the front edge to keep the wind off us. While building the wall, Ronnie's headlamp fell off and tumbled thousands of feet down the mountain. Anyone watching from below may have thought they were watching a climber fall to their death.

I sat down, hugged my knees to my chest, and tried to ignore the elements. Ronnie paced all night, back and forth on the six-foot long, two-foot wide ledge. At morning light, we looked down and saw a path below the cliff we had slept on. Getting down was easy. We ran down the mountain.

There is a hut at the bottom of the mountain, one guides and clients sleep in as they prepare to climb. We stopped outside it to rest and regroup. As we were, two guides came outside to check on weather conditions.

Because You Can

They found us casually sorting gear at their table and looked at us suspiciously. I hoped we were not in trouble for intruding.

"Aren't you cold out here?" one of them asked, "just sitting there without gloves on?"

"No," I said, "It feels quite nice here."

"Ah...." the other said, "You are those climbers who slept on the mountain. We could see your headlamp. Cold, No?"

"Yes," I replied. "Up there. Down here feels like summer camp."

The guides were impressed. They let us stay at their table and went back inside.

Luck Favors the Prepared

Finding My Way Through the Emerald City

I was on top of a mountain with two climbing partners when I shared an idea I had. I envisioned doing a traverse of all the mountains in the area. A traverse is where you climb one mountain, go down the other side, climb the next mountain, and continue until you have climbed them all. I wasn't sure if the idea was genius or ridiculous. Between each of the mountains were deep canyons, which, depending on the time of year, could be filled with ice-cold water.

At the same time, they both said, "It's not possible." They were quick and matter of fact about it, as if it couldn't be done.

For two years, I worked on a plan to do the traverse. I thought of what kind of gear I should take, what time of year would be optimal, and backup plans in case I got stuck. It was crucial to have a light backpack. I could not take a sleeping bag. I needed enough rope and gear to climb the difficult sections, but I needed to keep the pack light enough to climb some parts unroped, wearing the pack. I decided to take only one rope. That eliminated some backup plans. Most climbers take two ropes to make reaching the ground easier if you need to come down. One potential emergency exit would require 280 feet of rope. My single rope would only reach 100 feet. I wasn't going to carry a drill or bolts for anchors.

Because You Can

Between each mountain were canyons, some no one had been in before. It wasn't possible to predict how much water might be in them. Conditions change depending on how much it rains and the amount of snow that winter. Canyoners normally wear wet suits. I didn't have one, and I didn't want to carry one as I wanted to keep my pack light. I considered I might find myself like a wet cat without claws, slowing drowning in a bathtub filled with sandy, ice cold water.

I am inspired by Italian mountain climber Reinhold Messner, the first person to climb Mt. Everest without using bottled oxygen. That was in 1980. At the time, everyone told him he was stupid for trying. They said he would get brain damage and become a vegetable. He ignored their criticism. The naysayers had never climbed Everest. Messner was successful. He climbed Everest without bottles of oxygen and he did it by himself. My traverse was similar. It had never been done, and some said it was not possible. But with careful planning I expected I would find a way.

I patiently waited for the right opportunity. I wanted it to be after the spring snow had melted so there wasn't as much water in the canyons. I wanted it to be warm enough I didn't need a sleeping bag. Summer came and it was too hot. It was September when a cool spell arrived. Lower temperatures (85°F) were forecast to begin on a Tuesday. Anxious to get out of the house, on Friday, I drove to spend the weekend at my brother's.

Luck Favors the Prepared

I told my brother about my plans and waited for his response. His first impressions always help me gauge whether I'm planning something difficult or stupid. I told him my plan. It didn't faze him.

On his computer with its high resolution, I showed him what I intended to climb. Doing so made me have doubts. The bottom half of one of the mountains looked like a vertical maze of steep rock. My backup plan, if I couldn't climb it, was going down a narrow canyon that could be filled with water. My brother didn't seem concerned. In his mind, it was something I was capable of doing.

In the morning I left. It was onward to climb. My plan was to bivy (sleep in the open) at the base of Castle Dome, the first mountain. To avoid the daytime heat, I started hiking at 8 p.m., and reached the canyon at the bottom of the mountain at midnight. As I got close to the mountain, I found a place to sleep away from the water. It was midnight, quiet and peaceful. As I pulled things out of my pack to lay down, I noticed a flashing on the screen off my emergency satellite-based device. In bold, red, capital letters was the message:

SOS IN PROGRESS

Somehow, the device had turned on inside my pack, and then a button had been pressed to send an SOS. I pressed the power button to turn it off. It responded

Because You Can

with:
> SOS IN PROGRESS
> CANNOT TURN OFF UNTIL SOS IS CANCELED

I was in a canyon. To send a message, I needed better reception. I scrambled up one side as far as I could and tried to send a cancel again. At first, no luck. Then, I got the message:
> SOS HAS BEEN CANCELED

At the same time the SOS was canceled, I received incoming messages. The International Emergency Response Coordination Center had called my emergency contact when the SOS had been sent at 10 p.m. In preparation, they had called local authorities and the park service. Three parties were waiting until morning to stage a rescue — unless the SOS button had been pushed again. If that happened they would have gone in the middle of the night. Good to know the system works. But since then I have reverted to the old method of being safe — tell your emergency contact where you are going and when you plan to return. I don't count on electronic devices.

At first light, I stood up and started climbing Castle Dome. After getting over the difficult section, I put the rope in my pack and finished climbing to the top without taking the time to self-belay. I rappelled down the other side, into a canyon no one had been in before. I

Luck Favors the Prepared

Castle Dome Canyon

named it Castle Dome Canyon.

At the end of this canyon, I had to rappel into another canyon. When I got there, I couldn't see if my rope reached the ground or if there was water in the canyon. Not until I started lowering myself over the edge could I see that my rope barely reached the ground, and thank God, I landed in a dry section.

I walked in the direction of the next mountain, taking

Because You Can

The steep white face of Cliff Dwelling Mountain (center). The edge of Castle Dome (Left).

it slow, stopping to drink water. I never took water for granted. I had two bottles. When I came to a pool, I drank as much as I could, emptied a bottle, and re-filled it. There were enough obstacles to worry about. I didn't want running out of water to be one of them.

I continued toward the Crossroads, a junction at the bottom of the next mountain. This was my last opportu-

Luck Favors the Prepared

nity to fill my water bottles. I decided to wait to climb the mountain until I drank so much I couldn't drink anymore. Once I got on the mountain, there would be no sources of water the rest of the trip. I wanted to be prepared.

I looked at it — Cliff Dwelling Mountain. The wall was vertical. This was the spot I wasn't sure I would be able to climb, one my brother and I had studied on satellite images. I walked past the toe of the mountain, looking for a way to start up it. As I walked down the canyon I became frightened. The walls got steeper, and I saw pools of deep water ahead. When I stepped in what looked like dry sand, my feet sunk in like it was quick sand. I noticed a small ditch on the side of the mountain covered in tall vegetation. Desperate to go anywhere but down the canyon, I started scrambling up the ditch, grabbing on bushes and small tress to pull myself up. I couldn't see where I was going, but I knew it was going in the right direction.

When the vegetation cleared, I saw that I was on the side of the mountain where I had planned to be. I kept taking the easiest way, moving forward, and scrambled to the top.

I was the first dweller to sleep on the summit. It may not have been the best idea. I didn't have a sleeping pad and didn't realize how cold sand can get at night. I pulled my knees to my chest. It wasn't a position I could sleep in. After a few hours, I got up and found a tree to lean against, woke to the smell of ants crawling on me, and went back to the patch of flat sand where I planned to go down in the morning.

In the morning, I stood up and looked around. Suddenly I was dizzy. I stumbled, thinking I just needed a moment. As I fought to keep my balance, I became aware that I needed to drop to the ground before I fell over the edge. I turned away from the edge, saw a patch cactus, thought, *I can live through that*, and fell face forward into the cactus.

After recovering, I rappelled into a notch between Cliff Dwelling and the next mountain. One of my big fears had been that it might be difficult to climb up the other side. I found it was easy. I then climbed to the top of the last mountain, Lady Mountain. It had previously been climbed from the other side. An abandoned trail lead to its bottom, where there was a river and lodge. I just needed to go down it.

I thought that the way I felt was from my legs being tired. When you're scared you use your muscles more. But it may have been heat exhaustion. It was 92°F and sunny without a cloud. Rest and water were not enough to give me strength. I had this sense I needed to get down fast, even if it seemed I was doing the right thing by stopping to rest. Somewhere along the way, the rope fell out of my pack. I didn't notice it missing for some time. My pack still seemed heavy without it. I backtracked to look for it and then decided it was best to keep going. The rope was trying to save my life. Someone (my guardian angel) had taken it off of my pack, trying to lighten the load.

When I got to the river, I submerged my body and forced my head underwater. When I felt better, I got out and walked to the highway and the lodge. After lying under a big tree on grass outside the lodge for a rest, I left to care of business in the following order:

Call my brother and tell him I'm down safe.

Drink Gatorade.

Eat ice cream.

Buy a large Coke. It's a long drive home.

Creating Your Roadmap

How are you going to get there?

Think about how a roadmap looks. You don't just look at the end. To get to where you want to be, you go from city to city. Get a blank piece of paper. At the top, write where you are and the current circumstance. At the bottom, write where you want to be, who you want to be, and your goal. If your goal is to make more money, specify the amount. If it's weight loss, write your current weight at the top and desired weight at the bottom. If it's a new job, write your current one at the top and desired position at the bottom.

Because You Can

What resources do you have that you will need?

Make a list. This is your packing list. For my climbing, it is a rope, sleeping bag, and climbing gear.

What resources do you not have that you need to succeed? What can you do now to begin moving toward your goal?

This is your shopping list, the things to do now. An example might be getting gas and new tires. For my business, it was to write a new book, update my resume, and create a website compatible with current technologies. If you're not sure, write what are you pretending not to know.

Ask yourself what the first obstacle might be and how you will get past it.

It might be you can only drive 500 miles a day before you need to stop and rest. What kind of hotel do you want to stay in? Do you need to make a reservation?

It might be that waiting is involved. I often have to wait for good weather to climb a mountain. Specify what you need to wait for, when you expect it to arrive, and what will happen if you miss a window of opportunity. This helps set priorities. Keep your calendar open so that you're ready to pounce.

Luck Favors the Prepared

There are Exceptions to Every Rule

Although it's generally a good idea to plan for your future and consider the options as thoroughly as possible, for some ventures, this might not be possible. Not every venture will have a solid backup plan, and that should not stop you from starting. On the bright side, not having a backup plan is a sure way to inspire you to keep going. The music business is an example. Many successful musicians and songwriters will tell you if they had a backup plan, they would not have made it — they would have used that backup plan and never have succeeded. It's easier to take the backup plan when you're a starving artist.

Because You Can

Ask for Help

Refusing to ask for help when you need it is refusing someone the chance to be helpful.
- Ric Ocasek

Rock star Alice Cooper can hire anyone to play in his band, and he only hires those he considers A-list players. But you can't work in his band by simply by being the best guitar player on the planet. Cooper understands that it is just as important to get along off stage, so he picks players the band can tolerate spending time with.

If you lack expertise in an area, find partners with the skills you lack. Make sure everyone on the team is as passionate about the activity as you are and will not quit when you hit a bump.

I'm not sure why popular thought equates mountain climbing with leadership. On half of the mountains I climbed, we shared leadership responsibilities. Decisions were made as a unit. Look at a flock of geese. They take turns. When the lead goose gets tired, another takes over.

Perhaps the idea stems from mountains like Mt. Everest, for which most of the climbers pay to be guided. Those climbers are clearly subordinate to a leader who has climbed the mountain before. If it's a health aliment (cancer, for example), perhaps there are leaders (your doctors) who you should follow. Each circumstance is different. I encourage you to take responsibility for yours and contribute to the leadership required to reach your goal.

The Sedona Brothers

I had wanted to climb the Cathedral Spire in Sedona ever since I saw a picture of it in a magazine. Trying to find an experienced partner to climb it with was difficult. I hiked to the bottom with a real climber, one with the skills to get up it. Rain clouds were building as we reached the bottom and he worried that it might rain. He wanted to go somewhere else to climb, and I reluctantly agreed. It didn't rain. We would have been OK.

I have a motto to not try the same thing twice with a partner that quit on me the first time. Big Mike, the doorman at Long Wongs, a bar on Mill Avenue in Tempe, Arizona, was my next recruit. Mike had never rock climbed. Although Cathedral Spire had a reputation as being big and difficult, I wasn't worried. I didn't have a pair of climbing shoes that fit him, so he wore his Doc Martins, an English brand of leather boots. The harness I loaned him was a Chouinard alpine, basically

Ask for Help

a strap that went around his waist into which the rope was tied. It wasn't padded and was uncomfortable.

We climbed 400 feet up to a nice ledge. Things were going well when Mike asked if we could go down. He wasn't scared. He was smiling and having a great time. However, he had other priorities. Whereas mine was climbing, his was girls. He wanted to make sure that he got back to the bar that evening.

I have a rule, not to make someone continue climbing when they want to go down. I wasn't sure we could get down from where we were, though. The single bolt at the belay station was drilled in the 1960s. It protruded

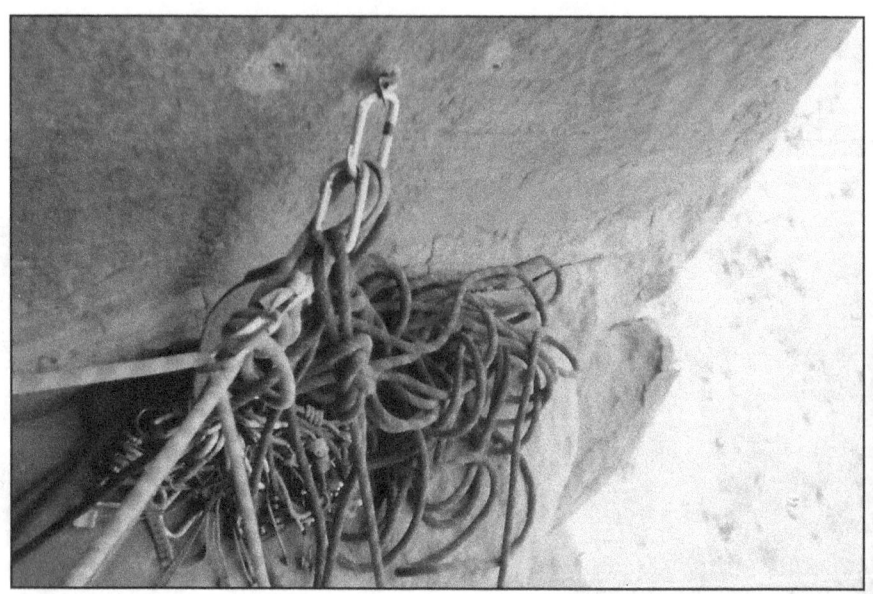

half way out the rock and spun in its hole, making it unsafe to use to lower ourselves. I saw it was possible to step sideways, through a gap between the tower we were attempting to climb, and its sister tower. I tiptoed across a ledge, squeezed though a gap, and was surprised and grateful to find a ledge so big we were able to unrope and walk around on it.

We took a break and enjoyed the scenery, I anchored the rope to a bush on the edge and wrapped the rope around it. I hoped the rope would reach the ground. It did, and we got down and back to town in time for Mike to enjoy his evening.

My younger brother was the next person I asked to climb the spire with me. He was not a real climber. He was an executive who went to the gym if he wanted a workout. We made it to the top. When I asked him how

Ask for Help

he was able to climb such a difficult climb when he had no experience he replied, "I thought I can't lose. My brother's not going to let me die. Let's get it done."

Transforming Uncertainty into Taking Action

People like to help. Be sure to ask for it from those you trust; they will be supportive and not too critical. Ask as many as possible. You never know who might be able to help.

My brother, Todd, following me on Cathedral Spire.

Main Takeaway
Don't be afraid to ask for help.

Because You Can

Expect a Few Bumps

An obstacle is an inspiration. A Pioneer is an Artist.
- Dangerous Dan

The difference between people who succeed and fail is those who succeed not only understand they will encounter challenges, they expect them. When they get to a bump, they already know how to make the decision to continue. They made it before they got started.

I expect going into a climb to be uncomfortable. When I get to a bump, I feel it's what I signed up for. It may not be ideal, but to get to my objective, I understand it's what I'm going to have to do. It seems that every problem has a solution. If they can land a man on the moon, I'm sure there's a solution to what you think is stopping you.

No Shoes

I have scars on the backs of my heels from blisters that never completely heal. I can't wear climbing shoes. I can't wear hiking boots without first cutting holes in the backs to relieve contact with my heels. I've tried every-

Because You Can

 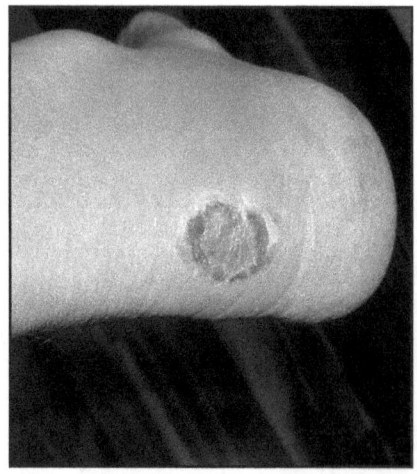

thing. Birkenstock sandals are the only footwear I can wear that don't tear the delicate scar tissue on the backs of my heels. When the tissue gets soggy from sweat, it tears. My feet are prone to infection. Nothing has turned up in blood tests except for anemia, a condition I've had for twenty years. The first time the scar tissue tore, two rounds of antibiotics were required. The doctor refused to give me more. Fortunately, I didn't lose a foot. I can't wear climbing shoes.

Bad Water

Most hikers like to filter water to remove dirt and bacteria. I don't blame them. But where I climb, water filters clog. I use tablets to treat water (kill the bacteria) and drink whatever else is in the water. On one climb, the

Expect a Few Bumps

only water nearby was a stagnant, green pool with frogs swimming in it. My choices were to drink the water or abandon my climb. I remembered that environmentalists say frogs are a good method for assessing how polluted water is. If it's good enough for frogs, it's good enough for me. I filled my bottles and apologized to the frogs for taking two gallons of their home. I promised to pray for rain. It rained the first night after I finished my climb.

So many people go into things with the attitude that it's going to be rosy and work because they have it all penciled out. Many don't have the flexibility required or haven't considered what they should do when they get to an unexpected obstacle. For those who have accepted they are going to face adversity, when they get to the green, moldy water, it is easier then to make the decision to drink it. They already made the decision. I had made

Because You Can

it before I left home.

I am encouraged by an experience I had climbing with an army solider whose job is teaching our troops survival skills. We got separated on the way down from a big mountain. I had no water to drink for a day and was dehydrated when he found me. He asked why I had not drunk from a swampy lake nearby.

"Would that have been OK?" I asked. "What if I got giardia?" (Giardia is a water-borne parasite that causes diarrhea. It can take a week for symptoms to appear.)

He laughed. "Hell yes it would have been OK! I can treat you for giardia. If you can't walk because you're dehydrated, there's not much I can do for you."

No Water

On July 25, 1931, despite the heat, Ronald C. Orcutt, tried to climb Cathedral Mountain. When he didn't return by dinner, the trail crew went on a search and found his body.

Following in Orcutt's footsteps, I found a new way to climb Cathedral Mountain. I expected it to take two days and left with two liters of water (a half gallon). Generally it's a good idea to drink that much each day when it's hot. I was carrying two ropes, a rack of climbing gear, and a sleeping bag. I couldn't carry more.

On the second day of my climb, I realized it was going to take longer than expected. It was 85°F and sunny.

Expect a Few Bumps

There was not a cloud in the sky. It was like being in an oven. I started to ration my remaining water to two cups per day, gambling that the top section of the mountain would be easier. I thought it might take as long to retreat as it would to keep going, and hoped I could finish the next day.

On my third day on the mountain, I wondered what the symptoms of heat stroke and dehydration were, how I would feel if I got them, and when I might know. I wondered if I might be too late to go down. I felt like a rabbit in the middle of the highway as it tries to decide which way to run.

The top part of the mountain was difficult. I fell fifty feet and hurt my shoulder. As I limped onward and upward, my eyes locked onto a target: a small tree growing out of the mountain, about thirty feet from the top. I thought if I could get to that tree, I could make it to the top. When I reached the tree, I wrapped a sling around it and clipped my rope into it. As I stepped off the tree, the tree fell out of the crack with my rope still attached. I was surprised it did not pull me off the mountain with it.

On the fourth day, out of water, I reached the top. The next morning I hiked down and reached my truck. I had climbed four days in 85°F heat with only a half gallon of water, something that's not supposed to be possible.

Because You Can

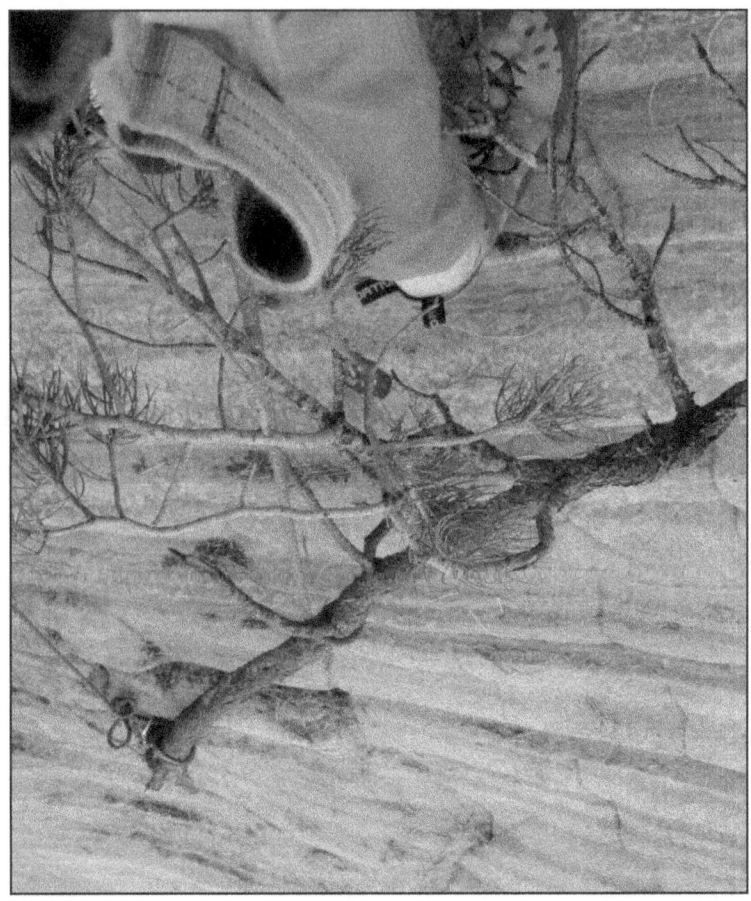

A small tree fell out of the crack it was growing in with my rope still clipped into it. I was amazed I was able to hold on and didn't get pulled off the mountain.

No Skin

There is a way of stuffing your hand into a crack, making a fist to secure it inside, and then pull yourself up. I

Expect a Few Bumps

was never very good at climbing difficult cracks.

My partner had climbed up first, was at the top, and began pulling the rope up as I climbed. There were no footholds. I stuffed my feet into the big crack. To move higher, I had to hang on my hands, swing my feet in the air, and place my feet higher in the crack. Then, with my feet stuffed in the crack, take my hands out of the crack and lunge them higher. Inside the crack, knobs of sharp granite crystals stuck out. In those days, you were not considered a hard man if you taped your hands to protect them. As I hung by my hands, sharp crystals dug into my skin.

Each time I fell, my partner lowered me to the bottom to try again. It was the 1980s, and it was considered bad style to rest hanging on the rope. If you fell you were lowered to the ground and to start over. I tried and tried but kept falling, tearing my hands to bits as my feet came out of the crack with my hands still inside it. I didn't want to give up. Eventually I had to. A deep hole was boring through the back of one of my hands.

I had to work that afternoon as a line cook. Part of my job was dipping ribeye steaks into hot a jus. It was torture, and I should have quit. I was wearing rubber gloves. Unknown to me, inside the gloves, my sweaty, moist skin was peeling off. By the end of my shift, the skin on both my hands was almost gone.

The next day, I saw my older brother and told him what happened. He told me not to worry, that my skin would grow back. The skin grew back without pigment. So now I have spots that cause people to think I have a disease. I have to be careful when I am outdoors to keep them covered with sunscreen or gloves. Otherwise they get sunburned, and small blisters form where the pigment is missing.

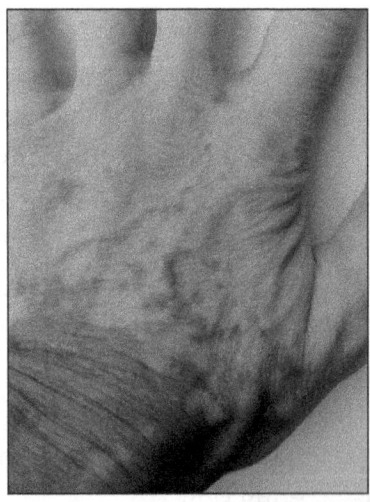

Creating Your Roadmap

A bump is something you can't go around. Other than planning and expecting them, there's no avoiding them. With the frog water scenario, I foresaw the possibility I might find limited water near my climb.

A bump might be, "At this point I'm going to be low on cash. I'll need to eat macaroni and cheese when it comes time to do payroll." It might be your goal is to lose twenty pounds and Thanksgiving comes in the middle of your map. When you get to that bump, perhaps you could deviate and be OK with eating more because you have planned to be ahead of your goal at that point.

Draw your bumps on your map where you expect them to occur. If you can't think of bumps, consider why you think it's going to be difficult to reach your goal.

Expect a Few Bumps

Softening the Bumps

As you create your roadmap, consider what you can do to soften the bumps. Refer back to the chapter "Luck Favors the Prepared." Plan backwards. Ask yourself what the first obstacle on your journey might be and how you plan to get past it. If the bumps are related to money, state the amounts and how you will acquire and spend them. Are there skills you lack, training you could benefit from, equipment that might help you succeed? Plan to acquire them on the map earlier than when you think you will need them. When you get to the bumps, remember that you already made the decision to accept them.

Permanent Roadblocks

Some roadblocks are simple. All you need to do is find a way over or through them. Some stay with you forever (illness, disability, scars), and you have to find a way to adjust to them permanently. No matter how you live your life, bumps will keep coming. Avoiding the things you want to do just to avoid them is pointless and futile.

Main Takeaway

Life is going to hand you bumps no matter what, so better to go through them then spend your life trying to avoid them.

Because You Can

Taking the opportunity to climb when I was in Oregon.

Take Your Opportunities

Do not wait for an opportunity to be all that you want it to be. When an opportunity to be more than you are now is presented and you feel impelled toward it, take it.
- Wallace D. Wattles

Take your opportunities when they present themselves. If you cease to act on them, God will stop presenting them. You can't plan for opportunities. When they present themselves, start. Those who are successful act when they see an opportunity.

It's My Party

I watch the weather in the three cities close to a mountain I want to climb. As my fiftieth birthday got closer, there was a small window before the last of the winter snow would melt. After that there would be no water near my climb. I wanted to go climbing. But to do so would mean being a no-show at my fiftieth birthday party. I called friends and family and, with hesitation, afraid I might dissapoint them, asked how they would

Because You Can

feel if I went climbing instead of coming to my party. To my surprise, they were not only supportive, they encouraged me to go climbing. It was their birthday present to me. I left to go climbing. They had a party without me, complete with birthday cake and displays of my baby pictures.

Getting to the mountains was not easy. I was carrying two ropes and a huge amount of climbing gear. It was all I could do to keep standing as I wobbled forward into the wilderness. With all the equipment, there was no room for water. I saw dark streaks on the on the north side of the first mountain I planned to climb. I got lucky and found water there.

Before I started, I had checked the forecast. My phone displayed sun icons for a week. That night, it snowed, my down jacket blew away, and hurricane-force winds make it too loud to sleep.

After climbing two unclimbed mountains, I packed up and moved. The next mountain was the sister summit to the Altar of Sacrifice. I hiked sideways across the bottom of it to look for the easiest way until I reached an impasse — a drop of 400 feet.

To continue, I tied both of my ropes to a tree and rappelled. I was excited to be on the other side of the impasse, and started climbing up the mountain. Unfortunately, when I was almost to the top, I saw the route I was climbing did not connect to the summit. A small bridge of rock connected the two summits. It looked

Take Your Opportunities

dangerous to cross, and I didn't have a rope. I had left both ropes hanging to get back up the way I had come down. I thought to myself, *You will die if you fall, the rock is loose and unpredictable, you don't know where you are going, and if you get to the top, you don't have a rope to get down.*

I wasn't sure what to do.

Then it happened. I started moving as if I was going to climb without a rope. I watched my body. It was like not being able to stop yourself from eating too many potato chips. Then, just as unexpected, something inside me decided to stop. I watched myself turn around and go back to look for another way.

I went back to camp. I was out of food. My rations the previous two days had been two goo packs and instant coffee — a total of 200 calories. I wouldn't have anything left for breakfast. My secret weapon was instant coffee with cold water when I was hydrated. Along the way I had accidentally sat on several cactus so I decided to try to eat one, something I found easy when you don't care about a few extra needles. Ants swarmed the trap I had my sleeping bag on. I got over it. I was exhausted.

The next day, I tried again, going a different way. Halfway to the top, I was gravely disappointed. A loose, broken face loomed, with no view of the summit. I felt it was getting too dangerous to belay (feed rope out to myself) using the normal method, so I abandoned tying backup knots. A backup knot would pull tight just as I would be in the middle of a difficult move, putting me at risk because I would have to stop, and using one hand, untie the knot so that I could move again. I didn't have the equipment to drill a bolt if I got stuck. It was getting late and I expected that I might not get down before dark. The way back to camp involved navigating a long and complex sequence of canyons. I would probably not find camp in the dark. But I didn't care. The summit was on my mind. I didn't want to have to come back again.

Just as I was about to concede defeat, things became easier. As I walked toward the highest point, the harsh wind turned calm. I smelled fragrant flowers. Instead of thorny manzanita bushes, I was greeted by gentle grass and flowers. Instead of loose rocks, there was as a path of paver stones welcoming me, beckoning me top the top.

I sat on top and enjoyed a peaceful place, one that had not been visited by humans before. I was in no hurry. The way I figured it, there was no way I was getting down before dark. I'd be sleeping in the cold somewhere. Why not on the top? I waited until I felt complete. Only then, I decided to try and get down while there was still light. I made it to camp just as it got dark. Dinner was a cup of coffee. It was my seventh day in the wilderness, and I had been out of food for two. I had climbed four previously unclimbed mountains. It was time to go home.

Take Your Opportunities

How to Get Time Off from Work

In the following story, it wasn't my fellow employees' business what I was doing (climbing) or for how long. The way my managers played it was brilliant. It was a win-win. But I had to take the initiative. My boss didn't know when conditions would be optimal to climb. I never expected my boss to come to me one day and say, "You know Daniel, you've been working hard. Why don't you take some time off and climb a mountain?" I didn't expect my boss to say, "I think the HR department can help you find a mountain to climb."

Some managers think they have to squeeze every hour out of their employees to get what they pay them. But working more hours only leads directly to success if you are an attorney billing by the hour. Successful managers lead more and time manage less. A good leader understands that when an employee needs time off for a personal goal, it's in the best interest of the company and the employee to find a way to make it happen.

Do not think, "I'm too important. They need me."

You do not need to be irreplaceable at work to be in the position to ask for time off. Thinking you are too important is an excuse to avoid the fear of asking for time off or what you may find when you get it. For some, work is their sense of identity. They will do "it" when they retire. Six months after they retire, they go back to work.

Because You Can

You, not your boss, must take the initiative.

Managers have no way of knowing who needs personal time, when, and for what. That's why it's called personal. Individuals need to take the initiative. The vast majority of people are too cowardly to ask for time off. Feel the fear and do it anyway. The worst that can happen is the answer is no.

Use sick days and personal time.

Sick time is the reward for being a reliable employee and coming to work each day. Sick time is something you earn. You earned the right to use it. Sick time includes days for mental wellness. If you feel burnt out and that it would be good for your mental health to go out and climb a mountain because the weather is beautiful and your partner is available, that's your prerogative. Not every manager will acknowledge this way of thinking; No company is going to go after an individual for inappropriate use of sick time.

Your boss needs to understand where you are coming from.

I have the mindset to not ask - just do it - use personal time if you run out of vacation. For those with the luxury of a work environment in which your boss is open to considering a leave of absence or time away from

Take Your Opportunities

work, don't tell your boss how it's going to be. Sell your idea. Be creative, as if selling a product. "You want to buy this, right?" Get your boss can empathize with you. It's not required that they have the same interest as you. Make it so they feel they don't want to be the one who stands in the way of making it happen.

Be firm when asking.

It might be your boss asks you to work longer hours for part of the week. In exchange for longer work days, you could ask for a shorter work week. "Well that sounds good, but I'd only be willing to do it if I had _____."

The Secret to Success is to Always Say Yes

I had only a week of vacation when I was asked by someone to climb El Capitan in Yosemite and by another to climb a new route on a famous mountain in the Swiss Alps called the Eiger. I had never been to Alp, so this was an opportunity. My potential partner was familiar with the mountain, knew how to travel in Europe, and knew where to stay. My ice climbing experience was minimal, while he was an expert. I considered what I should do — choose Yosemite or the Alps. I chose both. I purchased an airplane ticket to go to Geneva the following month and then left to climb El Capitan in Yosemite.

After climbing El Capitan, I returned and made an

appearance in the office. I wasn't sure how I'd deal with not having enough vacation time to go to Europe. I told my boss I was going and, as short as a week seemed for a trip to Europe, that I would be back soon. Before I left, I filled out the time sheet for the first week I would be gone using a combination of sick and personal days. I thought I'd worry about what to put as my time for the second week when I got back. I left for Switzerland. My partner, Ron, was waiting for me at the airport in Geneva.

In the middle of our climbing route, we came to a section of ice that looked difficult. Ron was the better ice climber and went first. I waited, positioned to hold his weight should he fall. He moved skillfully, stepping sideways across the steep ice. A thin layer of ice covered a layer of loose rocks the size of marbles. If the ice cracked, he would slide on the marbles and fall. As he got to the other side, where there was thicker ice, he yelled that I should start following him.

The rope between us was not clipped into any gear for protection. The ice was too thin to screw an ice screw into the ice, and the rock under the ice was too loose to hold gear securely. I was halfway across when I broke through the ice, lost my balance, fell backwards, and started sliding down the mountain.

Ron plunged his axe into the thick ice he was standing on and leaned over on top of it. I fell a hundred feet before the rope between us came tight. I got back on the

Take Your Opportunities

ice, kicking my crampons as hard as I could, and climbed up to meet him. We made it to the top.

After we got down, we went back to town and rested. I'd been in Europe less than a week and climbed what we wanted. We thought about what else we might climb. Ron wanted to climb the Strekchorn, a mountain that would require miles of hiking. To save money, instead of taking the tram up the bottom part of the mountain, we began an eight-hour trudge of a steep trail. We passed a hut we could have stayed in for $30 US. We trudged on, reached the glacier close to the mountain, and looked for a place to sleep. As we got there, Ron told me his knee was hurting and he would not be able to continue.

"Do you think you can solo that?" he asked while pointing at the mountain.

There were a lot of hazards to consider. I would have to finish getting to the mountain by crossing the glacier by myself and hope I didn't fall into a crevasse. I could get lost and climb something more difficult or have a difficult time getting down from the top. Mandatory 5.7 climbing was required, and I would free-soling, without a rope. I would really be putting myself out there. I considered things. It was Ron that wanted to climb it. In my heart, I didn't want to climb it enough to justify the risk.

"No," I said. "Let's go down."

As the climbing part of the trip was over. I decided to go to Rome. I'd never been. I took a small backpack and a collared shirt to wear inside the Vatican and boarded

Because You Can

the night train. When I got there, I walked the streets, seeing places the average tourist does not. I went to St. Peters' Square and did a tour of the Vatican. The next day I took a boat ride around Venice. Then I took a train to Milan and then headed back to Interlaken.

In Switzerland, from a pay phone, I called work in the states. I was relieved when I got the office answering machine. I left a message: "Hi, this is Dan. I'll be late getting back." Ron was ready to go home. We called his travel agent and got tickets. The hostel we were staying at had a big send-off party. In the morning, we left for Paris, the place we were to fly home from.

Take Your Opportunities

We checked into a hostel in Paris, close to the Louvre. As we sat outside the glass pyramid, a French newspaper photographer took our picture. For the next six days, we walked or took the subway everywhere. We visited Notre Dame and Jim Morrison's grave and hung out on the lawn next to the Eiffel Tower.

Back in the states, I wasn't in too much trouble. Although I had planned to be gone for a month, I had been gone for only two weeks. Some managers feared I was setting a bad example. Mine was ecstatic. I had put in hundreds of hours in unseen overtime and finished my projects earlier than expected.

Creating Your Roadmap

You can't plan for opportunities and may not be prepared with a map to follow when one presents itself.

Transforming Uncertainty into Taking Action

Knowing which opportunities are worth seizing and which ones to let slide is not something you need to worry about. Take them all. You never know where one might lead.

You generally can not seek opportunities. That's why I chose to go to Europe. If I passed up on that chance and tried to plan a trip later, I might not have had a climbing partner and had to hire a guide who would not have taken me to try a new route on the Eiger. I suspect it would have been years before I got around to it. I may never have gone.

Take Your Opportunities

Main Takeaway

Take your opportunities. All of them.

Because You Can

Start

Books are written one word at a time. Mountains are climbed one step at a time.

To succeed, you must take action. You must do something today to start moving toward your goal. Some self-help books say that all you need to do is think positive thoughts, and then you will receive what you want. The secret, they say, is not to think about what you don't want. They say if you keep holding positive thoughts about what you do want, then your job is done.

That's wishful thinking. If I only thought about climbing a mountain and never stepped foot on it, I would not reach the top. Rather, I have to go to a mountain range and hike to the bottom of what I wish to climb. Before I leave, I have to prepare by packing adequate supplies. When I get there, I have to begin, one step at a time, making the effort to climb to the top.

The authors of self-help books know positive thinking alone will not bring you what you want. The author of *The Secret*, for example, is said to have been introduced

Because You Can

to positive thinking after reading *The Science of Getting Rich* by Wallace Wattles. In his final chapters, Wattles emphasizes that positive thinking is not enough and that you must take action today:

> That he may receive what he wants when it comes, man must act NOW upon the people and things in this present environment. You must use your thought as directed in the previous chapters, and begin to do what you can where you are; and you must do ALL that you can do where you are.

The Alps Come to America

Sometimes the only way to get to the top of a mountain is to climb others on the way. It's called a traverse. The following is about a traverse of the mountains in an area of Zion National Park called the Court of the Patriarchs.

We knew we wanted to do a traverse of the mountains, but couldn't figure how to get started. Driving down the road, looking up at the mountains, they all looked steep and blank. There did not appear to be a way to get started. The first mountain didn't look like it could be climbed.

We parked the truck and walked along the side of the road in front of the mountain. Back and forth we walked. It was cold and we were discouraged. I suggested to my partner we get coffee at the lodge across

Start

the street. We were supposed to be hard men (tough climbers). It would be uncool to act like tourists. I had to twist his arm. We did not have anything else to do except drive home.

As we sat sipping coffee at a table on the second floor of the lodge, looking out a big window at the mountain, our waiter noticed our focused attention and struck up a conversation. He told us about the Old Mountain Trail, a path that ascends the otherwise blank face. It had been closed in the 1960s after several, including some fatal, accidents. He told us to be careful.

As soon as we exited the lodge, we ran across to the bottom of the mountain and tried to find the trail. We

found it in disrepair, with remnants of metal cables secured to the mountain with spikes. We had found a way to start. A one-paragraph note of our traverse was published in *Rock & Ice* magazine. I appreciate the blurb but felt like Jimmy Page must have when *Rolling Stone* magazine, not appreciating its significance, gave the first Led Zeppelin album a one-paragraph review.

Footnotes

https://en.wikipedia.org/wiki/Rhonda_Byrne. Cited on-line June 24, 2020.

The Science of Getting Rich. Wallace D. Wattles, 1910.

Rock & Ice Magazine. Issue 93. July, 1999.

Just do it

Start now. Do something, anything that will help you reach your goal. Success is not achieved with one big act; rather, it is achieved in the accumulation of many small and effective acts. When you put your power, intent, faith, and purpose into ever act you do, every action, no matter how big or small, is a step toward success.

Anything Helps

I was on the way home from a climb in the desert Southwest when I stopped to pick up a hitchhiker. He was a Native American teenager on his way to a city in which

Start

there was a store that sold craft supplies and leather. He was making stuff to sell and showed me what he had made: a bow and arrow and a tomahawk. I asked how much he wanted for everything. I gave him more than what he asked for and drove him to the store.

I waited while he got supplies and then drove him home. We drove for miles on unmarked dirt roads, deep into the reservation. As we got to it — a trailer on a hill in the middle of nowhere — there wasn't a tree in sight. Dust blew in the wind. I couldn't imagine being that isolated. I have a lot of respect for him. He was trying to do something to better his situation.

Transforming Uncertainty into Taking Action

Often a goal is so big and lofty that the amount of work required to reach it seems overwhelming. The solution is to break the journey into steps and to focus on each step, one at a time. All you have to do to be successful is get from one step to the next. Chunk it down. After planning, just start. Don't attempt to micro-manage everything before you get to the next step.

Main Takeaway

No matter how daunting a task might seem, just start.

Because You Can

Walking a tight rope (slack line) across a canyon gorge on a summer night somewhere in Switzerland.

Believe in Yourself

I'm looking for a lot of men who have an infinite capacity to not know what can't be done.
- Henry Ford, Ford Motor Company

In *100 Ways to Motivate Yourself,* author Steve Chandler writes about interviewing Arnold Schwarzenegger in 1976. Arnold was working on the movie *Stay Hungry.* No one in the restaurant they were having lunch in recognized Arnold. Steve asked him, "Now that you have retired from body building, what are you doing to do next?" Arnold replied, "I'm going to be the number one box office star in all of Hollywood." Steve asked him how he planned to do that. Arnold replied, "It's the same process I use in bodybuilding. What you do is create a vision for who you want to be, and then live into that picture, as if it were already true."

Believe it can be done. Believe you can do it. If you're in business, believe in your product and team. Some call this vision. I see myself climbing to the top, even when I don't have all the pieces of the puzzle figured out. I'm afraid on a lot of climbs. I am able to move past the fear because I have confidence in my abilities, I am prepared, and I believe in myself.

Small Miracles, Hummingbirds, and Blackberries

The last unclimbed mountain on maps of Zion National Park was Gregory Butte, named after a man who did a geological survey of the area in the 1930s. The bottom of the butte sits on a plateau level with the top of Kolob Arch, one of the longest natural arches in the world. There is no easy way to get to the top of the plateau. In August of 1954, Fred Ayres and A.E. Creswell were the first climbers to reach the top of the plateau. They climbed to it so that they could measure the span of arch. Gregory Butte remained unclimbed.

My effort to do the first ascent of Gregory Butte began in 2015 when a friend asked me, "Now that you've climbed the Altar of Sacrifice (one of the biggest and previously unclimbed peaks in Zion National Park), I suppose you are going to do Gregory Butte?" He assumed that since I had the technical skills, I would be a good candidate. I hadn't thought about it.

After exploring along the bottom, I did not see an easy way to get to the top of the plateau. Everything looked difficult. I believed in myself. I picked a place where there were cracks to climb and began. After several days, I gave up.

Believe in Yourself

Gregory Butte (upper left); Kolob Arch (Middle).

When I told my friend about my failure, he reminded me that there is a gully that comes down from the plateau, one used by those who climbed up to the plateau to measure the arch. I set out again to find the gully. When I found it, there was water running down it from snow melting. It was spring. I played hopscotch to place my feet on dry holds but didn't get far up it.

I returned in July. I left my house the day after the fourth, when there was a cool spell of 90°F. I was bored with city life and tired of the noise from neighbors set-

Believe in Yourself

ting off leftover firecrackers. Although water was not flowing, the gully was covered in a healthy, florescent-green moss. It was slippery and treacherous. This was my first encounter with the hummingbird. It hovered near my face, wondering who I was and what I was doing. I wasn't sure I was in the right gully. The rock was soft as mud. Near the top, the angle lessened, and I suddenly realized I was in the correct place.

I fixed my rope to a tree and made three trips back to the ground to get the rest of my gear and water. When I reached the top of the plateau, the hummingbird buzzed me again.

Once back to the top of the plateau, I walked around the bottom of Gregory Butte, looking for a climbing route that would go to the top. I wanted to find a way to climb it without resorting to drilling bolts. I agree with Reinhold Messner, the first to solo Mt. Everest without using supplemental oxygen, when he said, "Drilling bolts murders the impossible."

Although nothing looked possible, I believed I would find a way. I started where it was the shortest distance to the top. Standing at the bottom, looking up at where I had to go, I expected I would have to link a path of overhanging cracks, roofs, and blank sections and then negotiate around large blocks that clung to the side of the mountain as if they might fall off with the gentlest of touch. First, I had to go and get the rest of my gear.

It was a long hike from the top of the gully to the bot-

Because You Can

tom of Gregory Butte. It took me several trips to bring my ropes, sleeping gear, food, and water to the bottom. To prevent myself from over heating, I changed into a bathing suit. I walked short distances and stopped under every bush big enough so that I could rest in shade. I was going so slow I feared I might not finish the climb within the number of days allowed on my permit.

The first day of climbing I got only 200 feet, tied my rope to a bush growing out of the side of the mountain, and came down. I didn't have a portable ledge in which to sleep on the side of the mountain.

In the morning, I decided to go for it. I got an early start and thought, if necessary, I would sleep in my clothes, hanging from the rope. I knew the climbing was within my technical ability. Sleeping on the side of the mountain without sleeping gear or a big enough ledge would just be a bump in the road.

To my surprise and delight, the higher I got, the eas-

Believe in Yourself

ier things became. In the middle of the route I found a hidden, wide crack that faced sideways. It looked like a giant staircase, allowing me to fit my entire body inside it for safety. It was rather easy to ascend, and I made good time. Small miracle. I was able to climb to the top, going up what seemed from the ground to be impossible. Hummingbird meet me at the top.

Because You Can

It took me two days to get down and to the car. I made three trips from Gregory Butte to the top of the gully, and then went up and down the gully several times to get the gear to the hiking trail. I was out of food and on my last trip down the gully when I noticed a large blackberry bush. Hummingbird watched me pick it clean. I took my time. Why wait for what you think it should be. Enjoy the space to get where you'll be. Once out of the gully, I was back into direct sunlight on a hot, 90F summer day. My bag weighed eighty pounds. It was a seven mile hike, uphill to the car.

Postscript

I twice returned to attempt to put up a second route on Gregory Butte. Both times I didn't make it up the gully as I got scared and wasn't having fun. I blamed my lack of desire on the rock being slippery, even though the moss was drier than it had been on my first trip. I blamed it on the amount of work required. I wondered how it was possible that hummingbird and blackberries had come so easily the first time.

It was heart. My heart wasn't into subsequent attempts. Without heart, I was like a car not running on all four cylinders. Whereas the first time I had a childlike wonder about the adventure that lay ahead, what I would find, and what it would be like to stand on top of the

Believe in Yourself

mountain, I had no such enchantment on subsequent trips. The first time, no matter what the discomfort and uncertainty, there was no place I would rather have been.

A key reason I am successful on climbs is that I want to do them, not for fame or money, rather because I feel like it. The classic question that mountain climbers are asked is why — why do you climb? The answer is simple — there is no purpose. Climbing is knowing what's important to your heart without the need to have a reason to follow it. When you are confident, have skills, and follow your heart, you are a force to be reckoned with and can do things that seem impossible.

Feel the Fear and Do it Anyhow

Sometimes you may want or have to go it alone. It's a different inner experience and satisfaction to climb alone. You have more doubts, and it may take you longer, but your fate is in your hands. No one except you decides what you should do and when or if you should quit and turn around.

Mont Blanc

I went to Europe armed for bear, that is, bringing every piece of climbing gear I owned. I could climb the most difficult, biggest peaks in the Alps. Chamonix, France, has the biggest rock climbs in the Alps. It is considered

Because You Can

the birthplace of modern alpine climbing and was the site of the first Winter Olympics. That's where I went.

When my partners and I got to Cham, as it's affectionately called, I found out they were not into climbing. The next day, they left on a train top return to a hostel in Switzerland. I had two large haul bags of climbing gear and intended to climb something. I decided it was too big of an undertaking to climb a big rock face in the mountains by myself, so I turned my sights to climbing Mont Blanc. At 15,777 feet, Mont Blanc (White Mountain) is the highest mountain in the Alps. It's also one of the easiest.

I went to a local climbing shop to get information about the safest climbing route on Mont Blanc. I wanted to find the least hazardous path, the one with the least amount of glacier travel. When I asked a clerk in the shop, he began to shout that it was dangerous and that I should get a guide. French guides make their living guiding. It's a full-time, professional career.

I ignored the criticism. After explaining that I was competent, understood the risk, and just wanted to know the safest route, I asked again. The shop employee stood down and told me what I needed to know before going back to raving about how dangerous it was to climb by myself.

The route I planned to take went up and over the mountain. I planned to start on one side and finish on the other. I went to pack what little gear I needed. After

Believe in Yourself

packing, I took a cable car that stopped at the Cosmique, a hut in the mountains from which I would start my climb. The hut provided a sleeping pad. I slept in my cloths.

I got to the hut early and met two climbers who were planning to climb Mont Blanc the same way as I planned to. I enjoyed their company and asked if I could join them. They said yes. We made plans to get up early the next day. Mountain climbers normally get an early start. Early is 1 a.m. Crampons and ice axes stick better when it's cold. When the sun comes out, the snow and ice soften, making climbing more dangerous.

In the night the weather turned. A storm came in, blowing snow and reducing visibility to zero. I woke every hour to check the time. Finally, at 1 a.m., I got up, and put my boots and crampons on. No one in the hut stirred. No one was getting up. The weather had scared them.

I thought, *how hard can it be?* The easiest route is a steep hike in deep snow. The difficult part is knowing where you are going. I walked outside and closed the door behind me. I was alone in a blizzard. I put on my goggles. There were footprints coming down from the mountain in the distance. I started following them, a straight and narrow path, slowly gaining altitude. When I was halfway across, I turned and looked back. The lights from the hut had faded, obscured by falling snow.

After thirty minutes, the footprints became covered

Because You Can

with fresh snow. I could barely make them out. They were disappearing for another reason — the route went sideways. The route follows a series of big hills, as I call them. After some time, the footprints disappeared a second time. This time, it was correct to go straight up.

As it became light, I reached the difficult part. Just below the summit, the snow and ice had pulled away from the top, creating a chasm. It was dangerous just to be near it. The other side of the gap was higher. I would have to jump over the chasm, plant myself on the other side, and stick.

I waited a long time, not sure what to do. Finally, someone else showed up. Two German climbers leaped across the gap. Monkey see monkey do. I had the confidence to follow them. They did not wait.

The top of the mountain was flat and white. An icy blizzard raged. The wind blew cold ice crystals. There was an igloo someone had built on top out of blocks of snow. I considered going inside and waiting out the storm. I wasn't sure how long the storm would last or how cold it might get. After some thought, I decided to keep going.

I wasn't sure which way to go. In the storm I couldn't see which side was down. The summit of Mont Blanc is surprisingly flat, and directions are deceiving. As I struggled to determine the best way to go, the Germans sensed my fear.

"It is you who need a guide now," they said through

Believe in Yourself

the blowing snow.

Me? I looked at them with confidence. I was concerned, not scared. There is nothing wrong with healthy concern and taking your time to consider the options.

I closed my eyes and asked for help. I decided to go down the way I had come. I re-traced my steps, running and leaping down the mountain over crevasses and the chasm.

A short way down the mountain, I met a guide who was yelling at two clients in front of him. Contrary to what seems logical, it is not the most experienced climber who goes first — it is those who might fall. There

Because You Can

was a rope between the guide and his clients. The guide was swatting at the snow with his pole, checking for holes and crevasses as he came down behind them. If one of his client's were to fall into a crevasse or slip, an experienced guide, uphill and thinking fast enough, can plunge his ice axe into the snow and stop them from falling. If, on the other hand, the guide was to go first and fall, his clients would not be able to hold his fall, and they would all perish. As I ran past them, the guide, displeased, yelled obscenities at me.

The steep section soon flattened, and I stopped to rest. I came to a pass, a saddle between two hills. I wasn't sure which way to go. I didn't seem to go going back the same way I had taken. I thought I should probably continue up the other side of the saddle. It's always safer to stay high than to risk going down low toward the glaciers, which are moving rivers of ice. Hidden under a layer of snow are cracks, fissures, and deep crevasses. If you fall into one, don't expect to climb out. If you survive, no one will hear you scream for help.

I stopped and waited for the guide and his clients to catch up. It seemed rude to pester them, but I felt I needed to ask. When the guide reached me I said, "Excuse me. I am lost. Which way to the hut?"

"You Americans!" he yelled, "you always think you can climb by yourself. You need a guide..." He began lecturing me, a good licking of verbal abuse. When he was finished I remained silent. After some hesitation, he

Believe in Yourself

pointed with his pole. "It is that way."

"Thank you," I said.

I was off and running. Perhaps I should have stayed and offered to pay him to guide me. Then again, perhaps he didn't know where he was going either. Neither of us had come down the way we had gone up. I suspect that after I left, he realized that the way he pointed was not the correct way, and he and his clients went back up.

I plowed down in as straight of line possible. As I came to a flat section, the clouds cleared and the sun began to shine. The weather in the mountains is different from in the city. You can be at a cafe in town, sipping espresso on a beautiful day, looking up at what appears to be clouds around the mountain, unaware that it's dark and blowing snow inside them and that climbers might be fighting to survive.

As the stormed cleared, I saw the cable car and hut a half mile away. To get to them, I saw that I would need to walk, unroped, across a half-mile glacier. It was summer, so the glacier was split wide open with cracks and holes. It would be like walking across a minefield.

Fortunately, I found that the summer sun had melted the snow that normally hides the big holes and crevasses. All I had to do was step carefully across chasms, pay attention, and not lose my balance. I reached the other side of the glacier, the hut, and the cable car, alive.

Because You Can

Main Takeaway

Whether you think you can or think you can't, you are right.

Transforming Uncertainty into Taking Action

What are you good at that's not the problem? Use it. Some of my climbs would have been easier if I was comfortable going down canyons to reach the mountains. I don't like water. My forte is climbing up things. I will take the long way if I have more confidence to do so.

Consider what's the worst that can happen. I have nearly died climbing. The way I look at it, the worst that can happen in business is not so bad. So long as no one gets hurt, it's often only money at stake. I give credit to my grandfather. Whenever I saw him, he would ask what I was up to. If it was a misadventure, he'd ask me if anyone got hurt. As soon as I told him no, he'd say, "Then it's only money." His motto engraved in me two things: people are the most important element of success; and in the end, nothing else matters.

When the going gets uncertain, consider that you got yourself where you are, and you can get yourself turned around. When I get stuck on a mountain and can't reach the top, I think, *Daniel, you got yourself here; you can get yourself down.*

Believe in Yourself

Watch Your Language

Instead of	Say
I can't	I can
I'm not	I am
I need	I require
I'm confused	I'm seeking clarity on that
I failed	I obtained an outcome different from what I intended

Consider how you woke up. If you began the day thinking, "I have to ____," take a moment and start over. Cancel that thought and say out loud: "I intend to ____."

Monitor what you say throughout the day. Avoid statements such as the following:

- I have to
- I should
- I need to
- I am supposed to

Say instead something like the following:

- I can
- I will
- I intend to
- I want to
- I choose to
- I decide to

Because You Can

Fear Just Means Think Twice

It should not stop you.

Just when the caterpillar thought the world was ending he changed into a butterfly.

Fear is healthy. It's telling you to pause and think things through. It might stop you for a moment. It should not stop you from moving ahead if you are passionate about what you are doing, have confidence, and believe.

It's easier if you want to be where you are because you love what you are doing or must be doing it. If you don't have passion or a clear reason for doing the activity, then things may become more difficult (fearful). To move past fear requires confidence in yourself, and if you're in business, then this means having confidence in your product and company. When I'm climbing with a partner, I have confidence in our partnership. If you have passion, are prepared, and have confidence, you can move past fear and be successful.

Because You Can

Two Ropes Are Better Than One

Twenty years after trying, I came up with an alternative idea for how to climb a mountain spire that had eluded all efforts: instead of starting at the bottom, I would start in the high country and go down to it. A long and difficult canyon passes close to the spire before ending at an 800-foot waterfall. My intention was to reach the waterfall by hiking a trail in the backcountry to a point where I would leave the trail, rappel down a cliff, hike across a valley, and work my way through a maze of canyons toward the waterfall next to the spire. I would carry 800 feet of rope and tie the ropes to a tree at the top of the waterfall, go down the waterfall, and come back with climbing gear to climb the spire. I would do this, of course, when the waterfall was not flowing, in the fall.

I followed my plan and reached the waterfall. I tied the ropes to a tree, threw them over the edge, and started rappelling to the ground. To carry 800 feet of rope, I had purchased the thinnest rope sold. As I went down, I thought the rope was going to break. I got scared.

Safe on the ground, I thought, *that's it for me, time to give up.* It would be too dangerous to go back up the thin ropes, and I would be littering if I left the ropes hanging on the waterfall. I went to sleep in my truck on the side of the road to think about what I should do.

In the morning, I decided to go back. I emailed a local climber to see if he had time to go. Having a partner

Fear Just Means to Think Twice

might make it less scary. He had two days off from work but needed to ask his wife. Since he was married, I didn't want to put him at risk going up the thin ropes. I decided to replace the ropes with thicker ones. I drove to buy thicker ropes, slept in my truck, and at 1 a.m., began the journey all over.

I reached the top of the waterfall by going down from the high country, rappelling smaller cliffs, and navigating miles of canyons. I felt shooting pains running up

Because You Can

my legs and was thankful my knees held up. When I reached the waterfall, I tied the new ropes to the tree, threw them over the edge, and started down.

As I got closer to the ground, hanging in the air, I saw the new ropes were not long enough to reach the ground. I pulled up one of the old, thin ropes, and tied one to the end of the new ones. On the last rappel, my hair got stuck in the rappel device connected to my harness through which the rope was threaded. I was tired and desperately wanted to get down. I ripped out small bits of hair. At 5 p.m. I was back at my truck. My friend and I were supposed to go back the next day, but I had pulled something in my arm. When I put pressure on my fingers, a shock ran from my hand to my elbow. We made plans to return after Thanksgiving.

Fear Just Means to Think Twice

As the time got closer, the forecast after Thanksgiving called for snow. I decided to go the week before, and by myself. I hiked out to my fixed ropes, put ascenders on the bottom rope (ascenders are clamps that slide up, but not down a rope), got five feet off the ground, and stopped. I was scared. Safe as it might be with thicker ropes, it didn't seem natural.

I hung in space, ten feet above the ground, twirling in a circle, and asked myself, *why do something you don't want to, something you don't need to?* After a few minutes, I found myself coming down.

I was uncertain what to do. I went to town and had a pizza. At 4 p.m., I drove out of town. I called a friend in Sedona, Arizona, and told him I would meet him there. I was planning to go to my brother's house in Phoenix for Thanksgiving. I would instead plan to spend a few days in Sedona first.

As I drove toward Arizona, there was a lot of internal chatter and criticism in my head. It was 10 p.m. before I returned to a normal state. Suddenly, I found myself pulling over. I watched as I turned the truck around. I was going back to climb. I suspected I'd get scared again, waste a ton of gas, and drive an extra seven hours for nothing.

In the morning, I took my time and went for pancakes at a restaurant close to the mountains. I wondered if I had gone mad. The waiter asked what I was up to. I told him — I was there to climb, had ropes hanging on

Because You Can

a mountain waiting for me to return to go up them, but I would probably get scared again.

After eating pancakes, I drove closer to the mountain, unsure of what I was going to do. I parked and found myself going through the motions of packing my gear, when a couple parked next to me — Shawn and Taylor. They asked if I knew of any good hikes. I told them if they wanted to, they could follow me out to my ropes. They had street shoes, so I didn't expect they would make it that far. There wasn't a trail to get there.

To my surprise, Shawn and Taylor made it with me to the bottom of the waterfall and my ropes. Shawn held the end of the bottom rope so that I didn't spin and twirl in a circle as I went up. As I ascended, I didn't look down or up. Looking up or down only made me sad I wasn't at the top yet.

I made it to the top of the waterfall. It took all day. And there, I found a place to set up camp. Before going to sleep, I turned on my satellite communicator to text my friend I would not be meeting him in Sedona and to tell my brother I would not be arriving for Thanksgiving until the last minute. The device would not power on which was odd because I had charged it and sent a test message before leaving home.

My heart sank. *I'm not going down*, I thought. *I deserve to climb something.* I thought about what to climb. There were two big mountains that had never been climbed, along with the spire. I considered how dangerous each

Fear Just Means to Think Twice

The top of Princess Spire. The top of the spire splits into three towers. I returned to climb all three.

might be. The spire was the type of climb I could carefully inch my way up. I decided to climb it.

The next day I took rope and equipment and hiked to the spire. I couldn't carry all of the gear in one trip. After climbing as far as I could, I went back to camp. On my

Because You Can

The cliff I went down. I was 100 feet down it when a helicopter arrived.

way, I found a balloon on the ground with the word "Princess." I named the climb the Princess Spire.

On big climbs, every moment counts. Instead of relaxing in camp, I coiled the ropes I had used at the waterfall and moved them to where I planned to go down when I was finished — a dry spot, several hundred feet away from the waterfall, less steep, and hopefully less scary to go down. Unknown to me, as soon as I did not arrive in Sedona, my friend called the park service and reported

Fear Just Means to Think Twice

me missing. They had no way of knowing my satellite communicator was not working.

The next day, I climbed within thirty feet of the top of the spire. The rock was loose and the climbing difficult. As the sun was going down, I decided to wait to finish until the next day. I felt a sense of peace. Whereas before I had been scared, now I felt comfortable.

The following day I heard a helicopter. The pilot saw my camp. He couldn't see me. The side of the spire I was climbing was too close to the surrounding mountains.

 It took me longer than expected to get to the top. I took my time and made sure every piece of protection I placed was good. It was not a place I wanted to risk falling. After reaching the summit, I headed down and back to camp. I wasn't sure how long it would take to get down to my truck. No one had ever gone down the way I was planning to. I decided to camp another night. The emergency satellite device would still not turn on. I later learned it needed a software reboot, which required holding down three designated keys while turning the device on, something that was not in the instructions.

At the crack of dawn, I put it in high gear, hurried to where my ropes were piled, and threw them over the edge. I was only a short way down the side of the mountain when I saw it. I knew it was for me. Helicopters are not allowed to fly in national parks.

The chopper flew up and hovered so close I could see the pilot. All I could think to do was give the pilot the

Because You Can

thumbs up, OK sign. My ropes were tangled in a mess at my feet. I went back to untangling them to make it clear I was OK, situation normal. I didn't know those searching for me were carrying a body bag.

After reaching the ground, I started hiking towards the highway. I thought to myself, *this is either going to go really good or really bad. Just smile, be nice, and hope for the best.*

When I reached the highway, I saw an ambulance with a paramedic and a law enforcement vehicle with two park rangers standing next to it.

"Are you OK?" the paramedic asked.

"I'm a bit thirsty," I said. "To lighten my bag, I dumped my water out before coming down."

"Do you want a ride to your car to get some?" The driver opened the door on the back of the ambulance and put my haul bag inside it. I looked at the rangers who were standing quietly next to their vehicle.

"Do I have to pay for that helicopter?" I asked, trying to keep a positive attitude.

"We called it for you."

They let that sit for a moment before adding, "No, you don't have to pay for it." They were happy to see that I was OK, relieved I was not injured or dead.

The ambulance driver drove me to my truck. I was a bit casual, too tired to think. As we approached I said, "There it is. You can drop me off here."

"We have lights," the driver said.

Fear Just Means to Think Twice

The driver stopped in the road. We got out, and she set my bag near my truck. I had forgotten why we had driven to my truck — to get water. As the ambulance was leaving, the law enforcement officers pulled up and parked next to my truck.

I looked where I had hidden the key to my truck and couldn't find it.

"We have your key," one of the officers said.

"Oh, thanks." I wondered how they had found it.

I unlocked my truck and got a bottle of water. I drank, taking my time. I didn't know what else to do.

On the hood of a car next to my truck, the officers had laid out a laminated map marked with a black sharpie where I might have been climbing. It had canyons named I didn't realize had names, mountains named I didn't know had names. I wondered where they got the map. I thought it must be something they kept in the back office, a map used for special purposes.

The officers produced a notebook they found in my truck that contained descriptions of the gear that might be required to climb each of the mountains. They had been looking for clues.

"Where did you get that map?" I asked, trying to make small talk, still not sure on where this was going.

"It's yours."

It was a print out of the map I had drawn and emailed to my emergency contact. The rangers had laminated it and then marked with permanent marker on it, naming canyons and mountains based on what I had written in my journals. (If you ever wonder how a mountain gets named, this appears to be one way.)

"How hard do you think the climb was?" one of the officers asked.

"Hard to say," I replied. "Sandstone that rubs off on your fingers like sugar. Upside-down gear placements." The climbing was harder than what I was letting on. I tried not to sound cocky, as if I'd been climbing something dangerous.

Satisfied, the other ranger, said, "You know... we don't want to do this... we have to."

"I understand."

"Have you ever received a ticket here before? You can contest it or mail it in."

I tried to read the ticket the officer was holding in his hand. I couldn't believe what I was seeing. At the bottom was $100. I thanked them. Things were going really well. Perhaps this was a good training exercise. The place I was climbing was hard to get to. No one had climbed there before. A rescue had never been attempted there.

After making calls to family and friends, I started the long drive to get to my brother's for Thanksgiving. I would come back. I spent the next eleven months going up and down those ropes, climbing all the mountains in that area. Each time I went up the ropes I was frightened. To lessen the fear, I used both sets of ropes. It seemed to me the chances of two ropes breaking at the same time

Fear Just Means to Think Twice

were nil. I was still afraid. I guess you could say I'm afraid of heights.

Transforming Uncertainty into Taking Action

When you feel afraid, look at your roadmap. Read the boxes with the bumps and how you expect to deal with them. This will give you confidence. You are capable of moving forward; you're just afraid.

When necessary, stop to consider the options and the risk, and then make the best decision. Before you continue, thank the fear and ask it to let you know the next time you should pause to consider your state.

Reducing Fear in Your Life

When you wake up, write down what you worry is going to happen that day. At the end of the day, before you go to bed, write down what did happen. It likely didn't happen or wasn't as bad as you thought it was going to be.

Main Takeaway

Some fear is healthy. It's reminding you to take a beat and strategize before moving forward.

Because You Can

My brother, John, on an adventure with me.

What If

Don't stop thinking

Constantly wondering "what if" is one of the best things to have in climbing, business, and in personal affairs: what if what I am doing isn't good enough? I didn't do that, should I have done it? What is my competitor thinking and doing? It's helpful to be obsessive compulsive with the question, "Am I doing everything I can?"

When climbing I'm always thinking, *what if I this doesn't work? What if I can't get to the top this way?* I am constantly looking for other ways to get to the top, and thinking of how I will get down if it becomes too dangerous. This way, no matter where I am, I am able to remain confident.

If you're over confident, you won't have these kinds of thoughts and may find yourself stuck and afraid to continue when a curve ball arrives. Always be thinking of options and analyzing how to do something better and different. A lot of people don't do this. They have only one thing on their mind at a time. They don't do as well as they could. There's something to be said about lying awake at night thinking.

Considering "what if" is different from worrying. To worry means to have stress about what might happen. Those who worry are more concerned about impending doom than success.

Constantly be thinking new thoughts about how to solve a problem, confident that one of them will work, confident that you will have a contingency plan in the event that the path you are on needs adjustment. As you do, you will come to understand that there's no need to worry — you will find a way as long as you keep an open mind and don't stop thinking.

Creating Your Roadmap

When you create your map, draw a box after each step and label that step, "What if?" Leave these open. Do not fill them out until after you start. If you keep considering "What if" as you go, you can avoid being stopped by a sudden obstacle. It's similar to how you keep thinking as you are driving, "What if the next gas station is closed? Perhaps I should stop and fill up now."

Transforming Uncertainty to Move Ahead

Get gas when you can.

What If

Main Takeaway

Don't stop thinking.

Because You Can

Trust the Heart to Work with the Head

Use Intuition.

There comes a leap in consciousness, call it intuition or what you will, and the solution comes to you, and you don't know how or why.
- Albert Einstein

I have a feeling that I call getting a green light. When it seems dangerous and irrational but my gut tells me it's OK, I put the pedal to the metal and continue. Similarly, I turn around when my gut tells me to, even when there doesn't seem to be a logical reason to do so. That happens more often than you might think.

If you're in business, read the customer (the mountain). Discern (use intuition) when someone is not interested in your pitch and change course. Don't be stuck on what you've prepared. Don't go down a path the customer is not interested in following. Be willing to change the script. Weave a path. It's a constant weaving.

It's not just, "This is the script, this is what we're going to stick to." Understand as you go in that you're going to have to deviate. Like following a map in the mountains, the customer, or your situation in life, may not agree with your expectations. You may have thought you were going to go straight up, but you need to make a left turn before going up. Be willing to improvise and adapt. Expect you will have to do these things from the moment you start.

Liberty Ridge, Mount Rainer

The western part of the United States was going through a drought. It wasn't to scare people about global warming. It wasn't hot. There just wasn't any water. It hadn't rained significantly in three years. I decided to cool off and went to the Pacific Northwest to climb Mount Rainer. I intended to solo the route called Liberty Ridge. It was a twenty-four hour, 1,400 mile drive to get there.

The first order of business was to get a permit. To climb any route on Mount Rainer requires a permit. To climb something by yourself, solo, requires special, written permission. I went to the ranger's office to get it. There were two climbers in front of me trying to get a permit when I got there. The head climbing ranger was asking them questions.

"What happens if you fall into a crevasse?" he asked. (A crevasse is a wide, deep crack in the glacier, hidden

Trust the Heart to Work with the Head

by a thin layer of snow on top.) The ranger hung his head quietly and listened for their response. He seemed to sense they were not going to give him the answer he was looking for.

"I'll use my ice axe to climb out," one of the climbers replied.

"Nope." He waved them off without giving them a permit. "Next." He looked at me. It was my turn to be interrogated.

"What happens if you fall into a crevasse?"

"If I don't die," I began, "I will probably have broken a lot of bones. I'll be stuck and freeze to death. You may never find me."

After a short pause the ranger began to speak. He seemed satisfied with my response. He understood, that I understood, how dangerous falling into a crevasse could be.

"A few climbers die every year here," he started, "at least one or two we never find. The bergschrund will be your crux." (A bergschrund is a deep chasm where a flat glacier meets an ice cliff. You have to step, jump, or fly over the chasm and then climb the ice cliff on the other side to continue.)

"Other than that, you should find the route in good condition." He was giving me permission to try.

I went back to my truck and packed my gear. From the parking lot, I hiked to the place where I needed to leave the trail and go out onto the glacier. When I saw

Because You Can

the glacier I became concerned. It was a jumbled mess of ice blocks the size of refrigerators laying on a field of snow crisscrossed with deep crevasses. It was not the path I was expecting to have to cross it to get to the mountain. Although the rangers had given me permission and I was capable, my intuition, my gut feeling, told me not to continue. I took a second look, then turned around, hiked back to the car, and drove 1,400 miles home.

The following summer I moved to Oregon, where I met Evan, someone who had never climbed a mountain. He had posted a note on the bulletin board at REI that he was looking for a partner. I called the number.

The first mountain we climbed together was Mt. Hood. Instead of climbing the normal route, I convinced him to do something more interesting and difficult, the Cooper Spur. Although Evan had never ice or snow climbed, I wasn't worried. He was a fast learner and stayed calm under stress. He planned to be an EMT. If ever my life depends on it, I hope the first responder is as quick to think as Evan.

We drove to the mountain and slept in our car at a parking lot close to the trailhead. The trail was buried in snow. At midnight, we started hiking toward the mountain. The land was partially lit by half a moon. We didn't have snow pickets, stakes that can be driven into the snow into which a rope can be clipped, so we kept a

Trust the Heart to Work with the Head

rope tied between us in case the other fell.

After taking pictures on the summit, we started down. We slid down on our butts, like sledding. Halfway down we meet climbers who were on their way up. "Why are you coming down?" they asked. They thought we were retreating. They couldn't imagine we'd already been to the top.

The next mountain I took Evan to climb was Mount Rainer. The route I asked him to climb with me was Liberty Ridge. It's a classic climb that many climbers inspire to be good enough to do some day. Most spend years climbing other mountains first. Several of Evan's friends warned him not to let me take him on it. They told him I was being dangerous by recommending it to him, that he wasn't ready for it. I rebutted that the climb was not difficult. It is managing natural hazards such as weather, rock fall, crevasses, navigation, and finding the easiest way that make it difficult.

The normal climbing season starts in the late spring to early summer. In the summer a road is open such that you can hike halfway up the mountain, camp, climb the mountain, and come back to the same camp. We would be going the first week of spring when the road was buried in ten feet of snow. To climb the mountain, we would have to do what's called a "carry over." We would need to start on one side of the mountain and spend several days climbing to the top before going down the other side. It meant we had to carry all of our stuff with us as we climbed, including sleeping bags and food, and we would park a car on each side of the mountain.

We parked Evan's van on the one side, drove my truck to the starting point, and started hiking to the glacier that surrounds the mountain.

As we reached the glacier, a helicopter was taking off. We later learned that one of the climbers in front of us had fallen as he climbed off the glacier onto the mountain. He died on the flight to the hospital. I soon found out what was so treacherous.

I crossed the glacier, towing a rope for Evan to follow, and started climbing onto the mountain. Normally, when I get to the end of the rope, I sit down and anchor myself before telling my partner to start climbing. The ground on the mountain, however, was a loose mixture of rock pebbles and ice cubes. It was like stepping on marbles. Only momentum kept us from falling.

I kept moving and yelled to Evan to keep following. Later we learned

Trust the Heart to Work with the Head

that the climbing party behind us had an accident in the same place. There was another helicopter evacuation and another fatality, after which we were the only climbers

Trust the Heart to Work with the Head

on the mountain. That night Evan and I slept above the clouds, unaware it was raining cats and dogs below.

By our second night, we had almost reached the top when it started to snow. There was zero visibility and we were not sure which way to go. I refused to let Evan use the GPS he had brought. I told him he needed to learn how to use his intuition. It took patience, but we found the correct way to continue. It was getting late, and we decided to camp. We didn't bring a tent. I told Evan I did not want to carry one. I had a plastic shovel and scooped out a flat section in the snow deep enough to get the

Because You Can

wind off our bodies. We had foam mats and down sleeping bags. We were plenty warm without having to carry a ten-pound tent that would have slowed us down and made climbing more difficult. It could have made the difference in why we were able to climb the loose rock at the bottom where others had fallen and died.

The next day was tiresome, the snow chest deep. Evan commented on how fast I was going. If only he knew. If I slowed down I'd collapse.

On the summit, we pondered which way to go down. I picked a spot and started down. An hour later, Evan,

Trust the Heart to Work with the Head

concerned that we were not going the best way, suggested that we stop and have a look at the map. Hanging from ice axes on the side of the mountain, we discussed where we thought we were and the best way to get down. To his credit, Evan figured it out without using his GPS. He was learning to tune into his instincts. And he had good instincts.

We took the way he suggested, and things got easier. Then we came to a big ice cliff. I carefully walked toward the edge and peered over to see how far I needed to jump and what the landing would be like. Evan gave me slack

Because You Can

Evan on the descent from the top; this was the second time he'd ever climbed a mountain.

in the rope, and I jumped. I landed a safe distance from a crevasse at the bottom. Instead of jumping, Evan, to his brainy credit, walked around.

We ran down into the clouds. Fog enveloped us, turning the snow into a heavy, dark rain, so thick we didn't know where we were until we reached Evan's van. We didn't speak. We were too tired. There was nothing left to say.

Trust the Heart to Work with the Head

Transforming Uncertainty into Taking Action to Move Ahead

Watch for signs that it's time to be flexible and change course. Learn to trust your body. It knows what to do. Consider taking a yoga, martial arts, or dance class. These classes require movement without hesitation and thought. They are a good way to practice getting out of your head and allowing your body to make the right move.

Intuition and Guidance

Sometimes, we'd like to know our purpose, the direction we are supposed to be headed, and what exactly we should do next. Life, the journey, would be boring if we knew exactly how to get where we wanted to be. There'd be no adventure in climbing unclimbed mountains, that's for sure.

    I don't get clear signals on which way to go until I am deep into an adventure. It's as if I'm floating down a river (scaling a mountain), and if I think I should go to the river's edge, take a turn, try to open a door that's closed, or go through a door that's open, then that's when I get a feeling, an intuitive hit, as to whether what I'm thinking about doing is in my best interest. If we deviate from the course we are on, we know by how we feel if it's a good idea or not. Nudges keep us from going astray —

Because You Can

that way doesn't feel right, this way feels better. Other than that, it's full speed ahead.

When I want to climb an unclimbed mountain, I imagine myself at the top. I may see what I think is a way to climb it. I'm not stuck on taking that path. As I get closer, if I see a better way, I will take it. It's the end goal that matters. Along the way you have to be flexible, and use intuition to know when you might be placing an opportunity on a higher pedestal than it deserves.

Trust the Heart to Work with the Head

Know when to say, "No, this is not exactly what I had in mind. I think there's going to be something better around the corner." Know when to say, "Yes, this idea seems illogical but it feels right. I'm going with it."

Main Takeaway

Trust your heart to lead your head in the right direction.

Because You Can

Be Flexible

Adventure is allowing the unexpected to happen. How can there be an adventure if you use a guidebook to arrange everything beforehand.
- Richard Aldington

Jim Carey did stand-up comedy in nightclubs before he was famous. One night, the pressure was on to move his career forward. As he prepared backstage, he wondered what he would say when he got on stage. *I don't know what I'm going to say,* he thought, *but I know it's going to be OK. I know I'll figure out something.* Suddenly, he got an idea. He went on stage and just stood there, smiling and grinning. And as he stood there, people just started laughing. That fueled him to go into what he does best: improvisation.

To be successful, you have to think on your feet, be willing to change course, and change the script when needed. Few things end the way they start. Every journey requires some tweaking along the way. People get overly committed to a path. They may think, "OK, this is what we're going to do." They may think, "Well this is

Because You Can

what we're supposed to do." It may be all they know how to do, and then when something unexpected happens, they can't react. They may not think outside the box or haven't thought about the options. They might be over confident, stop thinking, and just continue until they get stuck. When that happens, they fail because they encounter something for which they don't know what to do. Or they move forward with their original idea blindly, eventually failing because they can't react because they stopped thinking about contingency plans.

If you're in business, you can have the greatest plan, but the market and customers may not agree with your plan. They will do their own thing. If you don't have flexibility, the ability to adapt and change en route, you're going to have a problem. On a climb, I often need to take a different path to finish what I started and reach the top. I still get to the top. In many cases, if I had said, "This is the way I am going and I'm not going to deviate," I might have failed. I might have died.

Triangle Peak

The shortest path to get to the top of Triangle Peak would have been going down a canyon filled with water. I'm better at climbing up mountains. The truth is that I was scared to go down the canyon. I have less experience going down canyons than climbing up mountains. I chose to climb Triangle Peak the long way. Some might

Be Flexible

say I wasn't being flexible. I was going with what my gut told me.

At the end of the first day, as I was taking off my boots, I noticed the back of my heels were red and flamed. The scar tissue from previous blisters was soggy from sweat. I thought they had healed. I was wrong. I had a pocket knife. I used it cut holes in the backs of my hiking boots. The issue was I would not be able to change into climbing shoes. I would have to climb everything in hiking boots. I hoped that was possible. I was at the bot-

Because You Can

tom of a 1,000-foot wall. I told myself not to step on any footholds that were not big and secure. No taking big risks.

After two rope lengths, I reached a tree. The way ahead looked long and scary. Instead of complaining about how far I had to go, I imagined myself sitting safely at the top. Vision, imagination, and positive thinking, slow and steady wins the race. I was carrying camping gear, a stove, and food for five days. The limiting factor was water. I could only carry one and a half gallons. At the end of the day, I reached an amazing spot and made base camp.

The next day I tried to climb "the triangle." I reached a small ledge where the rock wall above was blank. I swung around the corner to look for an easier way. What I found wasn't encouraging. Loose blocks clung to the side of the mountain. I lowered off the rope and went back to camp.

In the morning, I decided to go for it. I packed a bag with the remainder of my water. I left the stove and dehydrated food. I wasn't sure where I would sleep. I

Be Flexible

expected it to take two days to finish. A tree was growing on the side of the mountain. I thought if I could reach the tree, I could wrap my legs around it. It would be just for one night.

There were no cracks on the triangle into which I could place gear. An illusion of a crack was created by the shadows of loose blocks clinging to the mountain, ready to fall off at the gentlest touch. There would be nothing to clip the rope into. I wondered what I should do. I pretended to be Dangerous Dan. That meant I had skills. I just had to avoid being distracted by an inner voice that can take me into a spiral of negative thinking. In a moment, the answer came to me. It was no. I felt no.

The feeling meant I should go down. As much as I wanted to climb Triangle Peak, getting "no" caused me to feel good; not because it meant I could plan on eating a hamburger in town the following day; rather, it felt good being in a state where knowing what to do comes with ease. I decided to leave the mountain for someone else to climb, perhaps someone with a partner, or someone bolder than I.

I pulled the rope and started back to camp. On the way, out of the corner of my eye, I noticed the northwest face of the Sentinel, the mountain next door. I thought it would be nice to have some pictures of it and went to get a closer look. I didn't think I'd get far. The side of the mountain I needed to walk across appeared as if it might drop off at any moment.

Because You Can

I was surprised when I got to the other side and encouraged by what I saw. From that viewpoint, there appeared to be an easier way to climb to the top. Whereas a few moments ago I thought my attempt was a wasted effort, now I felt I was blessed.

The next day I went back with climbing gear. I needed to go as light as possible in order to climb the rock face wearing hiking boots. I left camp with a half liter of water, one power-bar, a windbreaker, rope, and a few

Be Flexible

pieces of climbing gear to use for protection.

It was 37°F in the morning and started to become windy as I climbed onto the exposed face. Instead of climbing straight up, I found that zigzagging away from my target and then back toward it worked best. I dragged the rope behind me. It wasn't clipped into anything. There wasn't anything I could clip it into. The sandstone was smooth and blank.

Near the top I became concerned. It looked like I was

heading for a dead end. The best holds would be if I climbed straight up, but it looked as if I'd get stuck if I tried that. As I reached the steepest part, I couldn't believe my eyes. To the side was a ramp with footholds leading up to the summit. I just had to keep my balance. There were no handholds. I made it to the top in my hiking boots and back to camp before dark. Success came taking the easiest way. It was so easy I had a difficult time getting record of it published. Publishers always ask how difficult a mountain is. If it seems too easy, they don't take you seriously.

Midnight Casino Mentorship

I was taking a break from climbing, thinking I had climbed all of the unclimbed mountains I wanted to climb (I was mistaken), when a friend with a kid in high school told me his son wanted to learn how to rock climb. His son went to a charter school at which juniors and seniors were required to do a "mentorship" program. They had to pick a topic that interests them, find a mentor who was an expert in it, and spend time each week doing that activity. They asked if I would mentor their son, Kevin, in rock climbing. I said yes.

School started in the fall. It was soon too cold to climb outside. By spring, I was desperate for something to take my student on. I chose the Pulpit, a six-hundred-foot peak in the Sandias near Albuquerque. It was April, so I

Be Flexible

expected the snow to be gone. My girlfriend, Willow, and her puppy, Seri —which means lucky— came with us.

We took separate cars. Willow drove with the dog and met Kevin and me at the top of mountain in a big parking lot. From there, I intended for us to hike down to the peak, climb it, and then hike back up to our cars.

We found the trail near the parking lot and started down it. It was soon buried in snow. We lost our way and found ourselves in deep snow and lost in the forest. I plowed ahead, got too far ahead of them, and sat down to wait for them to catch up. They were incredibly slow. I wondered if we would make it to the climb before having to turn around and hike back up the mountain.

When we got to the climb, the trail was clear of snow, and things were looking hopeful. Kevin and me roped up and started climbing the peak. We were a few hundred feet up when my internal guidance system felt we wouldn't make it to the top and back to the car before dark. Kevin was climbing well, but I thought that if we continued we'd run out of time.

It looked like we might be able to go sideways to a tree and lower ourselves to the ground to where Willow and Seri were waiting. Since it was a mentorship I wanted my student to participate in decision making. As Kevin and I reached an anchor, I asked him what he thought we should do.

"We're running short on time," I said, "I'm not sure we can make to the top while it's still light. We have two

Because You Can

options. Should we try and climb to the top or go down?"

"Go down!" he said without hesitating.

We went down and packed our gear to go home. I thought about how slow Willow and Kevin had been coming down the mountain. It seemed that if we all hiked back up the way we had come down, there was a good chance we would be stuck in the dark, in the snow, without sleeping bags.

"You guys," I instructed as I pointed to the trail, "hike down to the parking lot at the bottom of the mountain. When you get there, call a cab and go to the casino nearby. Take the elevator to the top floor. There's a fancy restaurant there. Order anything you like."

Be Flexible

They couldn't take a dog into a casino, so I was going to have to carry the dog through the snow back to the car at the top. I needed to go light. I gave Kevin the rope to carry.

"I will hike to the top," I continued, "with the dog and drive to the casino to pick you up and pay for dinner. Got it?"

They looked at me with blank faces as if I couldn't be serious.

"Oh," I added, "Kevin — when you get to the casino, call your mom and tell her you are safe. Tell her what we are doing."

We parted ways. I started hiking up the mountain; Willow and Kevin started hiking down it. I felt bad for the dog. I found myself climbing up cliffs and rock faces. I alternated from holding Seri tight in one hand as I climbed up something, to throwing her down into snow when I needed both hands to climb down something. Willow had told me not to let Seri off her leash. But the dog understood I was its only chance of getting home. She looked at me sad sometimes for the abuse I seemed to be giving her, but she kept following and allowing me to hold her when I needed to scale a wall.

Meanwhile, Willow and Kevin were not finding the trail down as easy as I had told them it should be. A section was covered with snow where it crossed a wash. They didn't realize the trail continued on the other side, and instead of crossing it, they went down the wash.

Because You Can

They got lost. They later told me they thought they were going to die. Eventually, they were able to make it to the bottom, where they called a cab and went to the casino. As Kevin got out of the elevator at the top floor or the restaurant, still carrying the rope on his back, a gentleman sitting at a table said, "You know son, there's an elevator. You don't need the rope."

Seri and I made it to the top and my truck. I drove to the casino with the dog. It took an hour to drive down the backside of the mountain, get on the interstate, and off at the exit for the casino. It was 10 p.m. when I got to the casino. The parking lot was nearly full. I parked in the middle between two cars and let the dog out to give her water. I put her back in my truck and walked to the entrance to the casino. As I pulled the front door open, three security guards stopped me.

"No dogs in the casino."

I was caught off guard. It was late, I was cold, wet, and tired, and hadn't thought they could see a small dog drinking from a bowl between two parked cars. I explained that I was only leaving the dog while I went to the restaurant to pay for Kevin and Willow's dinners. They took my driver's license and did a check. After fif-

Be Flexible

teen minutes, they let me pass.

In the noise and bright lights, I wandered around the bottom floor of the casino, looking for the elevator. There were no signs. When I got to the restaurant, just as I found Willow and Kevin at their table, part of the security force got off the elevator and approached us.

"I thought I told you to make it quick!" one snapped.

The host at the front desk wondered why security was being rude. While we waited for our check, the guard left. After paying for dinner, we exited the casino and started the drive — not home — to the parking lot at the top of the mountain. I had to take Willow to get her car. It took us an hour to get there. After dropping her off, Kevin and I started driving to his house where I had picked him up that morning. We were almost there when my phone rang. It was 1 a.m.

"Hello?"

"This is Kevin's mother. Is Kevin with you?" The tone of her voice hinted that she did not know what we had been doing.

"Yes... did he tell you what we were up to?" I asked.

"I got a text from him at 10 p.m. It said, AT CASINO WITH DAN."

Kevin had not called his mother. He had texted her. And his text did not tell the whole story. After we pulled into Kevin's driveway, I waited until I saw the front door open, let him get out of the car, and drove away.

Because You Can

Changing Your Roadmap

What did Kevin learn, other than going off without his mentor can be problematic, and not to text his mother from a casino? He learned that sometimes things don't end the way you thought they would, and to succeed requires being flexible and making spur-of-the-moment decisions as unforeseen obstacles are encountered.

Draw a box on your map after each "What If" step and label it "Be Flexible." Flexible steps are spur-of-the-moment decisions that you make as you observe conditions and have an intuitive feeling that you should change course. Fill in these flexible steps when you receive intuitive, gut feelings.

If you decide to be flexible and change course, write in the bumps and risks associated with changing course. The end destination is the same. It's not moving on the map. Connect the new steps to existing steps that are downstream on the map.

It could be that after leaving Cleveland, you stop in Oklahoma, where you decide to finish getting to Los Angeles by flying and leave the car parked at the airport. When you get to L.A., you will need to rent a car to continue the drive to the beach. A possible bump might be you forgot your driver's license at home and wonder if the rental agency will rent you a car when you get there. What will you do if they will not?

Be Flexible

Transforming Uncertainty into Action

Observe when it's time to react and do something different from what you have prepared. I'm a Taurus and can be stubborn. Sometimes it's hard for me to know when it's in my best interest to consider the alternatives and not to be overly persistent. It helps to get in touch with your body. Refer to the chapter, "Trust the Heart to Work with the Head." Use intuition, your gut feeling, to balance what your logical mind is thinking with your heart. I'm an engineer. If I can do it, you can too.

Main Takeaway

Sometimes life doesn't work as planned, but flexibility will help you reach your goals anyway.

Take Risks

If I knew my hand of fate, would I hesitate?
- Delmar Fadden. Died while soling Mount Rainer at age twenty two in the winter, 1936.

Risks should be considered as you plan and create your roadmap. I put risk at this juncture because as you proceed on your journey, opportunities and obstacles that you did not foresee may present themselves. Some are blessings while others are frustrating hurdles. Some have true risk involved.

Taking a risk does not mean you believe in yourself so much you jump off a building, expecting you can fly. Unless you're an experienced base jumper and have a parachute, you will die.

NEVER MAKE A DECISION WHEN YOU ARE AFRAID. Fear leads to poor choices. Worry interferes electrically and chemically with the brain. Consider the old expression, "Sleep on it." Step back, take a moment, and take a break.

Before you make a risk assessment decision, gather more information. What do you and don't you know about the situation and options for continuing? What could you use more information about? What might be considered a distraction and not helpful, thoughts that originate from a scared little voice in your head on autopilot. Write these down so that when they come up you don't have to reconsider them. Consider the benefits and potential consequences of each risk, and if there is a middle ground that splits the difference.

An example in climbing would be, "I feel cold. I am worried I might get hypothermia. How do I know? I'm shivering. Thank you brain, now let me check the temperature. Oh, it's 50°F. I'm going to ignore the shivering and consider that I am shaking because I am afraid. I'm going to take a deep breath and relax. I'll put on a wind breaker. I'm not going to put on a sweater because when I start moving I don't want to sweat."

The Difference Between Flexible, Getting over a Bump, and Taking a Risk

It's the difference between tactics — how you are going to do it — and strategy, the bigger picture. You might say, "I going up that hill." You have flexibility in how you do it. An example is adapting a sales pitch and not sticking to what you have prepared when you notice the customer falling asleep. The goal is the same. You're going to sell them the same thing. You're just going to take a different path to get there. You're being flexible. Risk, on

Take Risks

the other hand, is "How risky is this?" True risk is involved. The consequences could be significant.

Standing up for What You Feel is Right
Anything worth doing is worth the risk of doing badly.

If you did your first hike after 1995, you probably are not aware that charging fees to go hiking (pay a parking fee) is a new requirement. You might believe that the fees are used to maintain trails. I would have believed the same except that after the program was implemented, trails and parking lots got paved and bathrooms were installed, all of which costs more than what you pay to park. When I saw the Forest Service's new brochures, I wondered what "Challenge Cost Share partnership with the American Recreation Coalition (ARC)" meant. I was surprised to discover that charging fees for recreation is the brainchild of a group of corporations that want to privatize and concession public lands for their profit.

In February 1998, the President of the ARC gave a speech to Congress on how the Recreation Roundtable, Walt Disney, and REI had helped the Forest Service implement the fee program. In 1999, under pressure from its members, REI resigned. In 2004, due to public anger, Congress passed the Federal Lands Recreation Enhancement Act. It placed limits on where fees could be charged. According to the new law, fees could not be charged for parking, picnicking, horseback riding

Because You Can

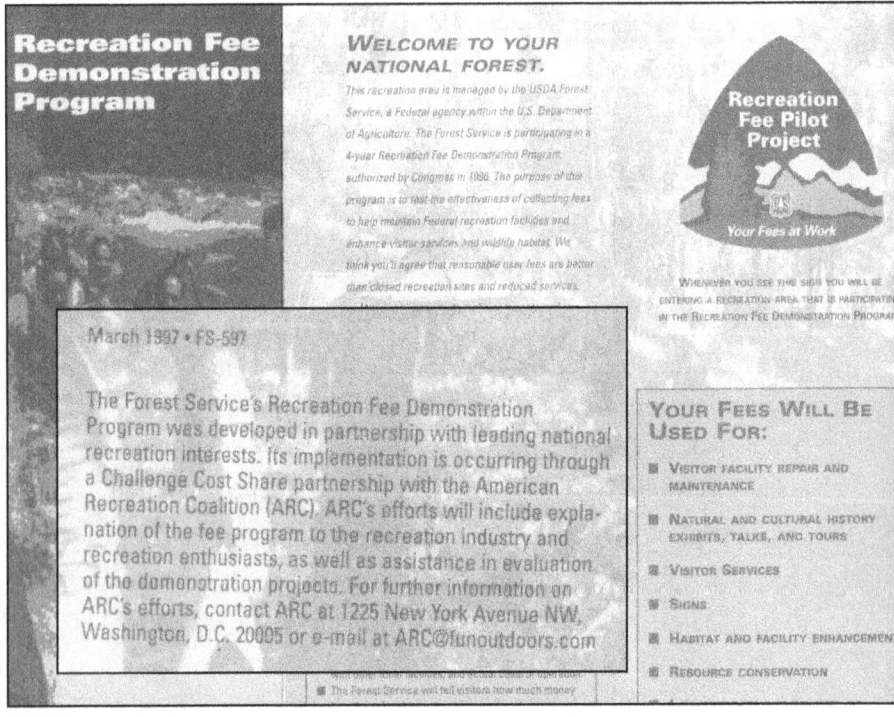

The American Recreation Coalition (ARC) is given credit on brochures the Forest Service originally published regarding the fee program.

through, persons passing through, camping at undeveloped sites, at overlooks, on public roads and highways, or for hunting or fishing. My student, James, and I parked where there were no restrooms. The sign marking the trailhead had fallen off and blown away years ago. A volunteer working for the forest service was parked nearby. When he saw us, he got out of his car and approached. I was focused on making sure I packed the

Take Risks

gear James and I needed to do our climb safely. The first thing the volunteer said to us was, "Are you going to pay the fee?" He was not interested in if we knew where we were going or had the proper gear to do a climb.

In addition to the lack of restrooms and amenities in the dirt parking lot, the law excluded me from paying because it was school project. I felt I needed to take a stand. James and I finished packing and headed off into the wilderness. When we got back, there was a ticket on my truck. The volunteer had called a law enforcement officer.

I took the ticket to court. I took a risk that the judge would find me guilty. The maximum penalty was six months in jail and a $5,000 fine. At the last minute, my attorney could not make it. I decided to defend myself. There was trepidation, tension, and fear in my body as the attorney warned me that the conservative judge would be prone to cut me off and not have patience.

James was allowed out of school and went with me. The Forest Service pulled out the stops. The prosecuting attorney and Forest Service support team took up half of the courtroom. James and I sat alone at a bare table on the side of the judge's desk, nervous and outnumbered.

When it was my turn to speak, I was like a deer in the headlights. I had been told by my lawyer who could not make it that the judge would be rude, harsh, brash, interrupt, and cut me off. I didn't have knowledge of procedure. I didn't understand that I present evidence

Because You Can

only after asking witnesses (the grippe volunteer) questions. I didn't properly, and at the right time, present those sections of the law that exempted me from being required to pay the fee. I had sent the judge and prosecuting attorney a detailed brief. I did not know if they had read it.

The judge found me guilty. Then, he cracked a smile, looked at James, and asked, "Son, did you enjoy getting out of school to come here?"

In a soft voice, James sheepishly replied, "Yes sir."

I waited for the judge to sentence me.

"Mr. Stih," the judge began, "I am fining you one dollar."

We were dismissed. James and I got up and walked quietly out of the courtroom. We took the elevator downstairs to the entrance. As we were exiting past the metal detectors, one of the security guards commented, "You were in there for a long time! It looked like you were going to make it." They had been watching on the courtroom video monitors. I nodded, appreciating their support.

The Forest Service may have read my brief. A few months later they took down the fee sign and stopped charging fees at undeveloped sites. For information on the history of outdoor recreation fees, see the websites for wildwilderness.org and westernslopenofee.org.

Take Risks

Sometimes Speed is Safety

It takes courage to move ahead when you're afraid. It's best to make up your mind and do what you decide before it's too late. Don't second guess yourself in the middle of a risky situation. Let go and do whatever it is you decided.

In 1998, my partner and I got the idea of fixing a rope down a waterfall to access an area in the high county from which to explore and climb mountains that had never been visited. We decided to reach the otherwise inaccessible location by climbing up, and then down, the other side of a mountain called the Sentinel. At the bottom we planned to go down a 700-foot cliff and leave our ropes hanging to return with more supplies.

The Sentinel was first climbed in 1938. We climbed it as they did in 1938, with little climbing gear. After reaching the top, we went down the other side, walked to the cliff we planned to use ropes to get down from, and stood at its edge. It was early spring, and a fast stream of cold running water was pouring over it. Water was not what stopped us from going down it. We didn't have enough rope to reach the ground.

We were faced with a dilemma. We had rappelled (lowered ourselves and pulled the rope) thousands of feet down the back side of the mountain. We had come down the north face, which had not been climbed before. We didn't have rock shoes or modern climbing gear to climb back up it. We could have waited for a rescue, but we didn't have a cell phone, so we decided to try to climb back up.

We were stopped halfway by a blank face. As I climbed onto a pedestal of rocks to get a better look, Ron asked, "Can you climb that?"

The boots I climbed a 5.11X, unprotected rock face in.

I didn't know. I ignored him. I believe in the power of spoken word. When you say something, the intention is reinforced. If I said, "No," it meant we would wait for a rescue. I didn't want to say anything until I was certain of what it would be.

Ron knew that if I didn't answer, there was hope. He looked for something to anchor himself to. He found a small bush, sat down, and tied himself to it. The bush, if it didn't pull out, would keep him from being yanked

Take Risks

over the edge. If I fell, I would go over the edge, continue falling 150 feet, and likely die on impact.

Standing on my tiptoes, I felt for a hold above my head where I could not see. I found one. It was small. After ten minutes of looking for a bigger one, I concluded it was the only one I would get. I was starting to get tired. I gripped the hold and pulled myself up to take a better look, placing my feet onto edges the width of a pencil.

I was on the rock but I couldn't see what was above me. I couldn't tell how difficult the climbing might be or if it was even possible. From where I was standing, it would be a long and bad fall. If I survived, I would not live for a rescue.

I remembered something a climber taught me when I was a teenager — speed is safety. Make up your mind and go. The longer you stay in one place, the more tired your arms and fingers become. If you stop moving, you will fall. It's better to give yourself a chance and make a decision. Come down or go for it.

In a moment, something other than my brain made the decision. I found myself moving up, without thinking, without knowing what I was putting my feet on. I pawed at the rock like a cat and just kept moving my feet as I scrambled to safer ground. I'm sure my guardian angel and a few helpers were giving me a boost. A psychic once told me, "In that case, he (Nick, my guardian angel) calls for reinforcements." If I fell I would have died.

The hardest part was a few feet from the top. By that

time, though, I was no longer scared. We retraced our steps down the other side and arrived at my van, minutes after dark.

How to Make No-lose Decisions

The secret to making no-lose decisions is to understand that whichever path you choose, you will experience, learn, and achieve things you would not have if you had taken the other path. Some of the mountains I climbed, ones that had never been climbed, I discovered when I was lost and failing as I was trying to climb something else. If you think you made a bad decision, consider what you learned and the positive events you experienced. Every choice helps us succeed.

There are a few things to help you realize the concept of no-lose decisions. The first is to remember that if you don't like a choice you make, chances are you can go back to how things were before.

Another is never make a choice because you feel you need to or should do something. If it's something you don't care to do, the likely reason you chose to do it is because you believe it will reward you with something better in the future. Understand what you're getting yourself into. Nothing is a sure thing.

Beware of the double-bind. When presented with a choice that seems to suggest it's "this or that," consider there may be a third option that you have overlooked.

Take Risks

Because You Can

A friend of mine thought what I meant by the secret to making *no-lose* decisions is not to fall or fail. She suggested I change the principle to "the secret to making *winning* decisions." I said thank you, but I didn't mean to imply don't fall or fail. I told her the truth: no one can tell you how to make a winning decision.

The concept of making no-lose decisions is that regardless of the outcome, you learn something and discover something new about yourself. You become that which you were not before. You should, therefore, be as excited about *not* making a winning decision as any. Don't worry! Do your best to make the best decision, and then quit thinking about it. After doing research and planning, you're wasting time dwelling on it.

Finally, as we say in climbing, take the easiest way. This is not to suggest you should be lazy. If your goal is to get to the top of a mountain and you know you can there by hiking a trail instead of spending several days climbing its steepest face, choose the hike.

To sum it up, whether you choose chocolate or vanilla, remind yourself that you're lucky you have choices and be grateful you're getting ice cream. It's going to be good either way.

Creating Your Roadmap

Add steps on your map where you expect to take a risk. As you reach a risk step, you may have new information

Take Risks

you did not previously have. When you get there, consider what you know and do not know about the current situation and the options for continuing. You might choose to create an alternative path that lowers the risk, or you might decide to go for it. Remember to consider if there is a middle ground, a third choice you overlooked or that was not previously available.

Main Takeaway

Sometimes you have to take a risk to continue.

Because You Can

If You Keep Going You Will Get There

Everyone's thinking of the destination
But the journey is the destination
Why would you keep waiting for it to get there
When you can enjoy the space to get there
Maybe once you get there it's boring...
Maybe it's the end
Just getting there is the wonderful part
- Donovan

If things look uncertain on your journey toward your goal, keep going. Often the way to the top only becomes visible when you get close to it. Until you are stopped dead in your tracks, have faith and keep going.

The Mountain Called Death Point

The view from Death Point is said to be one of the most beautiful and impressive in all of Zion National Park. As late as the 1970s, it was possible to get there by a combination of four-wheel drive roads and strenuous hiking.

Because You Can

Although it's inside a national park, the land bordering it is private property and now closed to the public. Landowners are serious about keeping trespassers out. The climb I did is now the only way to get to the summit.

My first attempt did not end well. I started hiking in the late afternoon. It was hot, 90°F. I took my time. I stopped to drink when I reached a creek on the way. I should have stayed longer and drank more, but the creek was swarming with white flies that bit me like I was in hell. The flies were the result of heavy and late rainfalls. It was painful, especially because I was wearing a bathing suit. My sweaty, juicy thighs must have seemed like a Thanksgiving feast. As I hurried along I almost stepped on a rattlesnake.

That night, I slept as close as I could get to the mountain without getting too far from the river. I needed to refill my water bottles before I continued in the morning. The next day I reached the bottom of Death Point.

I was feeling off. The heat made me exhausted, and things slowed to a crawl. By 9 a.m. I had only climbed 100 feet up the mountain. I considered that when I got to the top, I would have to walk several miles across it before rappelling a thousand feet to the ground to get back to my truck. That would come at the end when I would be exhausted and could make a mistake. I decided to retreat and turned around.

Turning back wasn't easy. It was 100°F, and I had forgotten how I got to where I was and how difficult it had

If You Keep Going You Will Get There

been. I knew if I reached the trail at the creek, I would be safe. Then I discovered blisters on both of heels. I stopped and covered the blisters with toilet paper and duck tape, but it was painful to walk. With each step, I felt the back of my shoes rubbing on raw flesh. I reached the trail and creek. From there, I walked seven miles uphill to the car in the afternoon heat. The bugs had no mercy. Large pieces of flesh were missing where blood dripped down the back of both of my heels.

I went back in October when the weather was cooler. I obtained a permit for five nights, more than I could possibly need. I left the car at 4am. To be sure I would not get blisters, I cut holes in the backs of my hiking boots. There had been no rain in ninety days, so I didn't count on finding water at the bottom of Death Point. I carried two empty two-liter soda bottles and filled them at a creek on the hike to the mountain. One gallon. That would be my supply of water from that point on. Some say that you should drink half a gallon each day. I wasn't sure how difficult the climbing would be, and planned to cut that in half to stretch my water to four days.

At the bottom, I found my gear as I had left it months earlier, along with a Cliff Bar in the pile. I wondered where the map was. It showed the way down once I got to the top. It was a good thing that I had memorized it. I found that I had left a full bottle of water. Although it was three months old, it tasted better than the water I

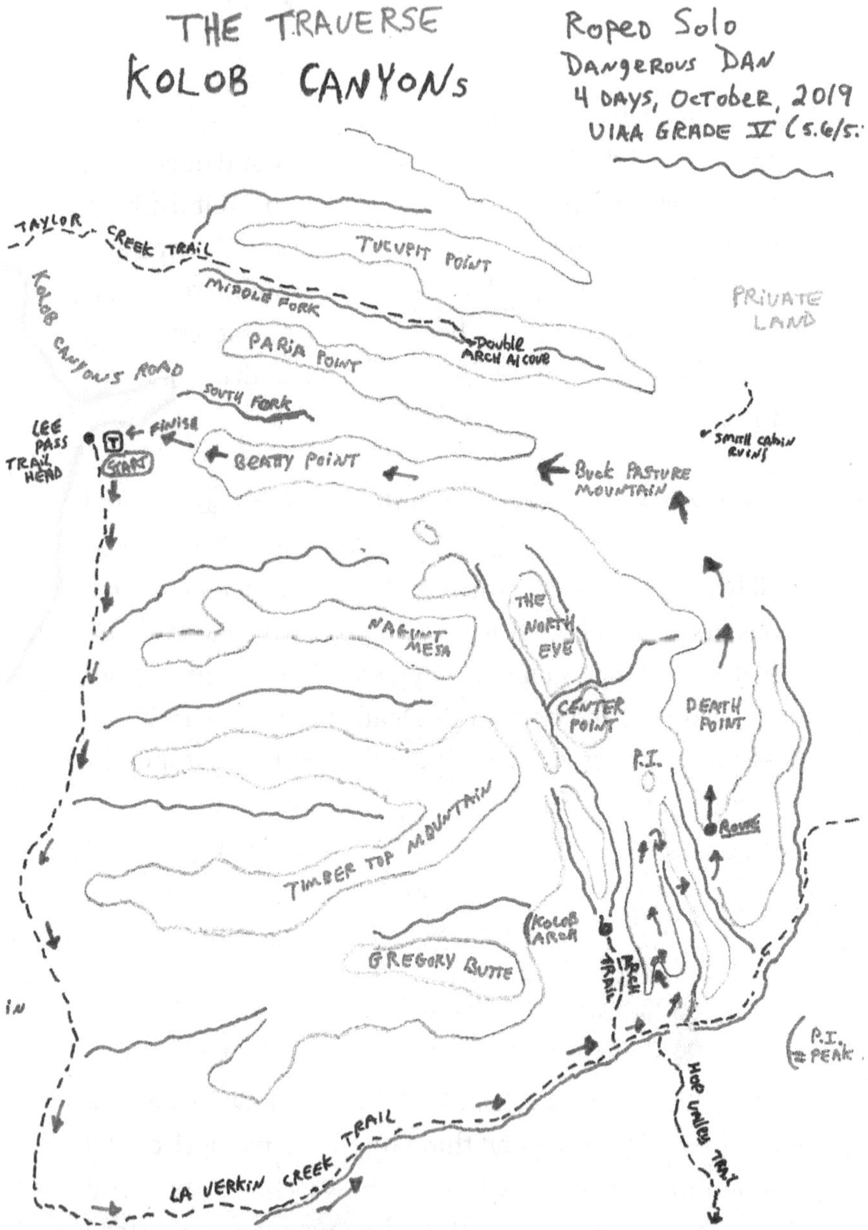

THE TRAVERSE
KOLOB CANYONS
Roped Solo
Dangerous Dan
4 days, October, 2019
UIAA GRADE V (5.6/5.
TAYLOR CREEK TRAIL
TUCUPIT POINT
MIDDLE FORK
PRIVATE LAND
KOLOB CANYONS ROAD
PARIA POINT
Double ARCH AlCOVE
SOUTH FORK
LEE PASS TRAIL HEAD
T
FINISH
START
BEATTY POINT
BUCK PASTURE MOUNTAIN
SMITH CABIN RUINS
NAGUNT MESA
THE NORTH EYE
CENTER POINT
DEATH POINT
P.I.
ROUTE
TIMBER TOP MOUNTAIN
KOLOB ARCH
GREGORY BUTTE
ARCH TRAIL
P.I. PEAK
HOP VALLEY TRAIL
LA VERKIN CREEK TRAIL

If You Keep Going You Will Get There

had collected at the now slow-moving creek.

I got the rope out of my pack, tied it to a tree to self-belay myself (feed the rope out), and set off to see if I could climb without wearing climbing shoes. I could. I climbed up to the sling I had tied around a bush I had used to lower myself on my previous attempt and went past it. The day was off to a good start.

The next day, I got the feeling to look down and saw a grasshopper. They say the grasshopper is the symbol of good luck. It's ability to connect to and understand sound vibrations is a symbol of your inner voice telling you to trust it.

Toward the end of the day, I got to a ledge big enough to sleep on. It had a divot in the middle to keep me from rolling off it. Although it was only 4 p.m., I decided to stop. I was tired and needed to rest. More importantly, I wanted to enjoy the space. That's one of the reasons I climb.

Although things seemed to be going well, I didn't know if the route I was climbing went to the top. There was a chance I'd get close to the top and find the last part blank, rotten, and impossible to climb. If that happened, I would have to go down. Once in a while I took a peak around the corner to see if there was an easier way. The rock on each side dropped off. I was lucky to have chosen the way I did. When I was starting at the bottom, I had almost decided to take a different way. Then I remembered not to second-guess myself. *You choose this*

Because You Can

way for a reason, I thought, *stick to it.*

As I got closer the top, I saw what I had envisioned — a single path that led to the summit. On either side were vertical, impossible-to-scale walls. I had made it. I didn't feel death. I felt an endless, needless suffering to what I was doing.

The plan was to walk several miles along the edge of the top of the mountain, along a series of flat tops that form a horseshoe. At the end of the shoe, I would rappel 1,000 feet to the road where I had parked my truck.

I thought the hike would be easy. Instead, I found the brush tall, thick, and sharp. It took great effort to move through it. It was a slow and painful trek. By 4 p.m. I was exhausted and on the verge of crying when I saw a clearing and decided to camp.

I unpacked and looked forward to the moonset. I tended to my feet, mended holes in my pants and shirt, and built a wonder-woman bracelet by wrapping duct tape around my arms. It was to protect my arms from bleeding as I forced my way through the bushes the next day. Dinner was a bag of Turkey Jerky. I had one energy bar and two goo-packs left, energy snacks with 100 calories of sugar and caffeine. It was the amount of water I had left that I thought of the most. I had been drinking almost half a gallon a day, more than my ration. In the middle of the night I got hungry and ate the energy bar.

The next morning started in good spirits. I wanted to get moving while it was cold so that I could wear my rain

If You Keep Going You Will Get There

jacket and gloves to protect my arms and hands as I battled through the sharp bushes. It was heartbreaking to see how far I had to go. I spent the entire day bushwhacking. The only thing that kept me going was the thought I had to. No one was going to rescue me. The end point wasn't moving on the map. As long as I kept moving, I would get there. If I didn't keep moving, I felt I would lie down and die, perhaps never to be seen again in the thick brush.

Near the end of the day I reached the top of a mountain called Beatty Point. At the bottom was my truck. It looked so close. But carrying a heavy pack, tired and exhausted, it was difficult and dangerous. As I carefully

Because You Can

made my way down, I came to a spot where I thought I should use the rope to rappel and lower myself. I set the rope around a bush, put the rope though my rappel device, and put my pack on. As I put weight on the rope, I heard a snap. The main branch split in two. I decided to climb down without using the rope.

At 4 p.m., exhausted, I stopped at another sleeping spot. I made a flat spot on the pointy ridge and drank my last cup of water. There would be no breakfast or water tomorrow. I was glad I stopped. As the sun went down, a group of hawks played in the wind, circling above. I strained to stay awake and not miss the show.

The morning started in good spirits. But I soon realized the epic might be far from over. I felt like a pilot

If You Keep Going You Will Get There

trying to land the space shuttle. I had spent a year studying photographs of the mountain from different angles and was certain on which ways not to go down. I knew where I should aim for: a place I could hopefully get down with one rope. My pants had big holes in the seat. My shirt was torn to shreds. I was out of duck tape to patch them. Yet it was full speed ahead. I wondered why I was being mean to myself. I had to keep my wits and focus on two things: not falling off the mountain (the rock was loose, and I was wearing a heavy pack) and choosing the best way to go. If I went the wrong way I would be stuck. If I didn't pay attention, I could go off the end of my rope. I wondered if I might collapse of thirst. There seemed no point to the pain and suffering I was putting myself through. It felt like a marathon, but there was no race to win.

At one point, I found myself at the end of my rope, stuck on the side of the mountain. Fortunately, there was a small crack into which I was able to place a piece of gear, and I was able to lower myself to a ledge that I walked across to easier ground.

According to the photos I had studied, I remembered I needed to avoid the temptation to go straight down, as big cliffs, too tall for my rope to reach the ground, were hidden lower down. I hiked sideways to where I expected to find shorter cliffs. When I got there, I panicked and almost cried. It looked as if there was no place my rope would reach the ground. The highway looked close, but

Because You Can

I didn't see a way to get there. If I kept going sideways it looked as if I'd be funneled onto a blank face with a huge drop. That's when I noticed them. I was practically standing on them.

Just as I was about to concede defeat, I looked down

If You Keep Going You Will Get There

and saw three old, rusted bolts. They were fifty years old and in better shape than some new bolts. There was a piece of strap tied through them from which previous climbers had threaded their rope. They had probably climbed up Beauty Point, the mountain I was going down. The strap crumbled when I pulled on it.

I couldn't tell if my rope would reach the ground. The previous climbers may have had two ropes. But I had no option. Not until I stood on the edge, ready to lower myself, could I see that yes, my rope was on the ground. Hallelujah!

Although I made it to the ground, there was still a maze of cliffs to navigate through to reach the road, and I was worried. I had cramps. The salt tablets tasted so bad I spit them out. When I reached the highway I was beaten and broken. As I walked to my truck, I promised I would do something nice for myself.

Sometimes It's OK to Stand Down

If you've done the best you can, having to call it quits is not the end of the world. Don't beat yourself up over it. Odds are that you learned something that will be pivotal to success when you try again. Sometimes our intuition takes over and tells us that we need to step back, and that's okay.

When my partner and I did a traverse of the mountains called the Towers of the Virgin, on our last day we came face to face with an unclimbed mountain called the Meridian Tower. I was too tired to give it 100%. I clawed at the bottom but couldn't get off the ground. I waited while Ron went to look for an easier way. He came back and said it couldn't be done. For the next ten years, I planned to go back to climb it. When I returned, I got lost. Twice. That led to a sequence of me finding more unclimbed mountains and climbing them. Ten years later I was successful.

Creating Your Roadmap

Add timelines to your map. Write down when you expect to reach each step. If you were driving from Cleveland to Los Angeles, you would probably specify cities as stopping points and which days of the week you intend to reach them.

Transforming Uncertainty into Taking Action

Follow your map! Believe in the map. Each day, commit to one action toward completing your goal. Don't forget to reward yourself along the way.

Main Takeaway

Sometimes the only way to make it to the end goal is to keep pushing forward, even if it seems impossible.

If You Keep Going You Will Get There

Because You Can

Be Thankful

*Love's lost for some small detail in the story.
Heart is what it's all about.*
- Donovan

I frequently give thanks for the opportunity to climb mountains and for my safety. There have been times I have nearly died climbing. None where so many things had to happen to prevent it as the following story tells.

Donuts, a Car, and a Song

In two weeks I had driven 3,000 miles for work. When the time came to go climbing, I got a few more calls and drove ten hours to El Paso through snow and rain then back home, where I picked up my climbing gear and started driving to the climb. I stopped to do more work on the way. I slept in my car. I was tired when I got there.

    The mountain I wanted to climb was in the middle of a maze of canyons, sandwiched between other mountains. I hiked toward the mountain with a bag full of gear. I had to climb a dead tree leaning against a cliff to get to

Because You Can

it. At the top of the cliff was a plateau, across which I hiked to get to the mountain.

I climbed the tree by leapfrogging a strap around it like a log jammer. I was halfway up when the tree started to move. The bottom was stuck in dirt, a foot away from the edge of another cliff. The tree would have fallen over if not for a small bush and the pile of rocks it was leaning on.

After getting to the top of the cliff, I walked to a living tree, put the rope around it, and rappelled to the bottom to get my bag. This is when the first of several things occurred that would be responsible for saving my life. The rope got damaged while dragging my bag up the cliff. I made a mental note that when I climbed, I needed to start with the other, undamaged end of the rope.

The next day, I started climbing the mountain. I climbed only 100 feet before I felt I needed to go down and rest. It didn't seem like I was that high up. I tied what I thought was the middle of the rope to a bush. The "ground" was a plateau the mountain sat on. To the side was a 700-foot drop into a canyon. The easiest way to climb the mountain had been to start from the plateau and tiptoe out onto a face that fell into the canyon below. As I went down, I needed to swing back onto the plateau.

To be safe while rappelling, I use what's called an auto-block. It's a method of wrapping a thinner cord around the rope and clipping it to your harness. Thin cords bind when wrapped around thicker rope. If you

Be Thankful

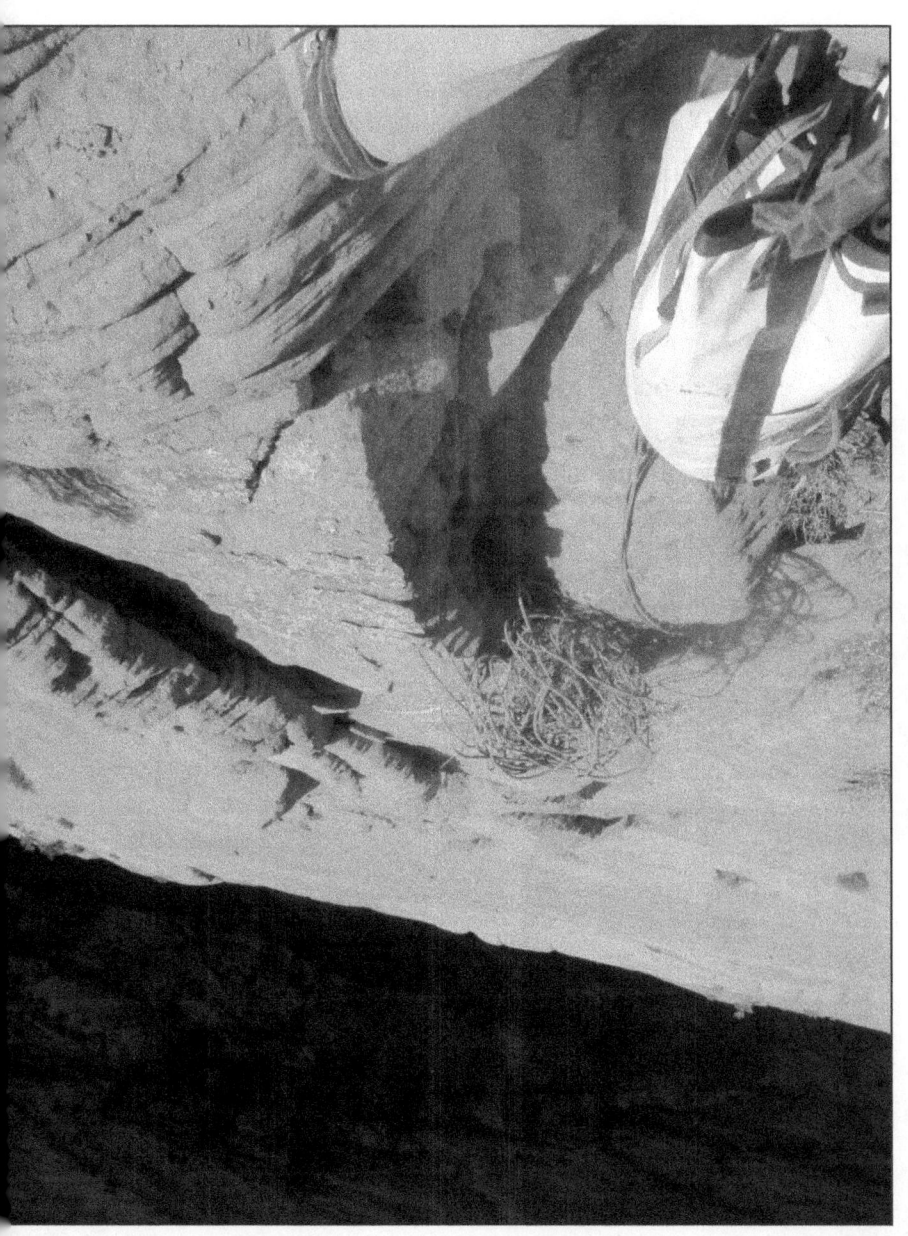

Because You Can

lose control, the cord will lock onto the rope like a helping hand. The heat generated from friction can cause it to melt, and it's good practice to periodically replace the cord. I had just bought a new, thicker cord. I looked for it on my harness and couldn't find it. The older, thin cord was there. It would have to do.

As I lowered myself, I kept looking up to make sure the rope wasn't running over a loose block on top that could fall on my head. I was almost to the plateau when the cord locked up and would not slide. Still looking up, I tugged on the bottom of the rope to feed it though my rappel device. I needed twenty more feet of rope so that I could swing around the corner. Below was a 700-foot drop into the canyon. It's not unusual to have hiccups, and for the cord to lock up. Still looking skyward, I cursed, hanging on the rope, unable to move. Finally, I looked at my brake hand, which was holding the rope, to see what the problem was. I was at the end of the rope! I had nearly done what John Christensen had: rappelled off the end of my rope.

When God decides an intervention is required, God doesn't budge. The thin auto-block cord was binding so tightly around the rope that it was stuck on the sticker the manufacturer had placed on the end of the rope. The rope would have pulled through my rappel device and I would have fallen to my death if the cord had not caught on the sticker. Had the sticker not been there, the rope would have pulled through. Had the sticker been on the

Be Thankful

very end of the rope instead of a few inches before the end, it might not have caught as it did. The rope I was climbing on was eleven millimeters in diameter, thicker than normal ropes. Had the rope been thinner, the cord I used might not have caught the sticker. A friend had given me the rope. It was twenty years old and had been in his closet since he quit climbing. He didn't expect I would use it. Had he not been home, had I not stopped to visit him, I would have used another, thinner rope.

Because You Can

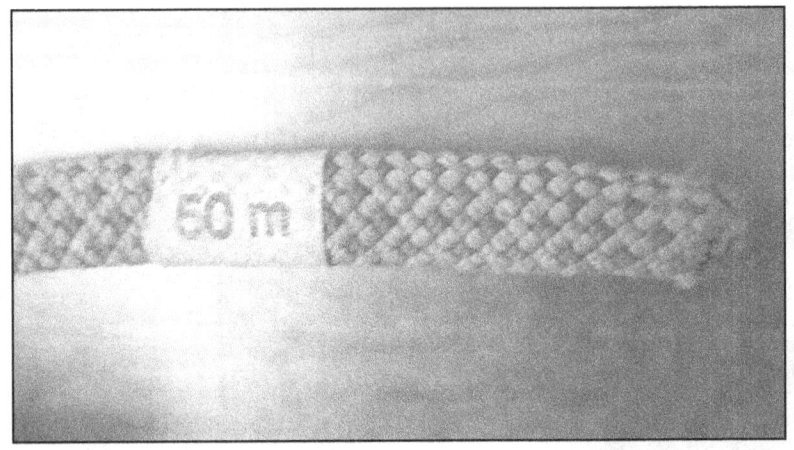

With one hand and all my strength, I grabbed the rope above my head and held on. On big climbs, I keep a jumar, a clamp, attached to my harness on a short leash. I reached for it with my other hand and put it on the rope. Saved.

As I hung there, I asked why I was alive. The list came quick. I'm OK with simple things. There were three things. The first was to bring the staff at the store where I get my mail some donuts. The second was to buy my nephew a car. He was eighteen and had been putting off getting his license because he didn't have a car. The third was to record a song I wrote with friends.

On the way back to my truck, at the top of the cliff at which I had to climb the tree, I found it. As I was rappelling down that cliff, I noticed something clinging to its side that looked like trash. It seemed odd, as only a handful of people had ever been where I was. When I got

Be Thankful

close, I found it to be the new, thicker auto-block cord I had purchased. If I had used it, I might not be alive. Did I drop it? More likely, my capital G, guardian angel, took it off my harness when I wasn't looking.

You might think the incident would have caused me to go home and stop climbing. It did not. The day after the incident, I decided to finish the climb by sleeping on the mountain overnight. I took a sleeping bag, one liter of water, and two energy bars. I reached the top the following morning. As I stood on top and looked around at the beauty surrounding me, feeling grateful for my safety, I said out loud to anyone and anything listening:

Thank you!

Because You Can

You Can Have More Than One Dream

You've just read a book about climbing. Climbing is just one of the things I do. I'm also a singer-songwriter. I've lived in Nashville, performed at the Bluebird Café, even did a concert with Donovan. I've worked as an engineer, a problem-solver, and a mold inspector — all while finding time to go climb more mountains.

I'm not rich. I'm not special. I just refuse to believe the lie that you have to pick one path, wear one hat. You can have more than one dream. You can live more than one life in the same lifetime.

Do the things you want to do.
All of them.

Because you can.

Creating Your Roadmap to Success

Get a blank piece of paper. At the top, in the center, write where you are, putting down your current circumstance. At the bottom, write where you want to be, your goal. Leave lots of space. If your map is longer than one page, put the goal at the bottom of the last page.

Step 1. What resources do you have that you need to succeed? Make a list. This is your packing list. For me, this includes packing a rope, sleeping bag, and regardless of how nice the weather is, a rain jacket.

What if? In place of the next step, draw a box and label it "What if." Leave it open. Do not fill it in until after you start. Consider "What if" as you go, similar to how you keep thinking while driving, "What if the next gas station is closed? Perhaps I should stop and fill up now."

Be Flexible. Draw a box after "What If" and label it, "Be Flexible." Flexible steps are spur of the moment decisions

Because You Can

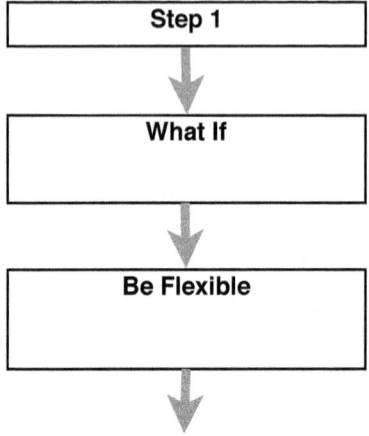

you make as you reach them. These will be completed as you go, whenever you receive intuitive, gut feelings that you should change course.

Expect bumps. Draw a box after Be Flexible and label it, "Bump." Fill it in with a potential bump. If you can't think of any bumps, consider why you think it's going to be difficult to reach your goal. A bump you might be, "At this point, I'm going to be low on cash. I might need to eat macaroni and cheese when it comes time to pay my employees."

You can soften bumps by working backwards from the goal as you complete your map. Are there skills you lack, training you could benefit from, or equipment that would help you succeed? Put in steps to acquire these before you think you will need them.

Creating Your Roadmap to Success

Risks. Draw a box after Bump, and label it "Risk." Consider what a risk might be at that point. When you get there, gather more information about the conditions and consider all the options before deciding.

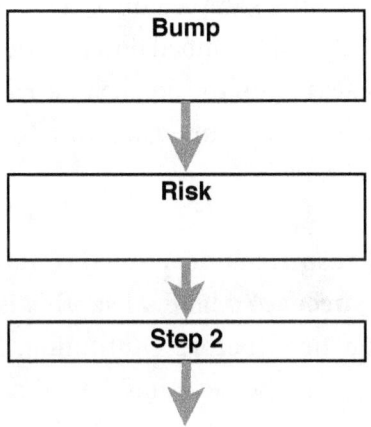

The Difference Between Flexible, Getting Over a Bump, and Taking a Risk

It's the difference between tactics — how you are going to do it — and strategy, the bigger picture. You might say, "I am going up that hill." You have flexibility in how you do it. An example of being flexible is adapting a sales pitch and not sticking to what you have prepared when you notice the customer falling asleep and not interested in what you have to say. The goal is the same. You're still going to sell them the same thing. You're just going to

Because You Can

take a different path. Being flexible is, "My gut tells me to do this instead."

Risk is "How risky is this?" True risk is involved. It might be that when you get to that point, you see a less risky way and choose to take a different path than what you planed. As an example, on one climb, the risk seemed too great, and I climbed down. When going back down, I saw (backing up to "Be Flexible") a way to walk sideways where I found an easier way to climb to the top.

Step 2: What resources do you NOT have that you will need to succeed? Make a list. This is a shopping list, things you need before continuing. An example might be getting gas and new tires. For climbing, it might be to buy a new helmet and gloves. For business, it might be to create a website compatible with current technologies. Before drawing Step 3, add boxes after step 2 for each of the following: What if, Be Flexible, Bump, and Risk.

Step 3: What can you do now to begin moving toward your goal? If you're not sure what the next step is, write what are you pretending not to know. For my business, it was making new connections on social media sites as I waited for my website to be completed. If waiting is involved, specify what you need to wait for, when you expect it, and what will happen if you miss a win-

Creating Your Roadmap to Success

dow of opportunity if you're not ready when the time comes.

Finish your map. Continue adding steps until you reach your goal. Each step should be preceded by a What If, Be Flexible, Bump, and Risk box.

If you keep going, you will get there. Add timelines to the map. Next to each step, write when you expect to get there. Be sure to remember to reward yourself each day along the way as you take action to reach your goal.

Creating Your Personal Roadmap to Success
The Dangerous Dan Way

Start → **Step 1** → **Consider What If** → **Be Flexible** — Pay attention to current conditions. Be ready to adapt. → **Expect Bumps** →

Look ahead in order to be better prepared for what's coming.

This is an opportunity to change course

You can not go around a bump. You may choose to quit.

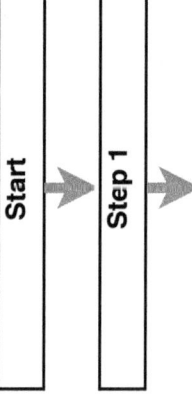

Taking this path changes everything. Use a pencil.

There may be new bumps and risks encountered. Draw them in.

Risk
You have choices.
Gather information before making a decision to move straight ahead or take an alternate path.

→ **Step 2** --→ **Step** → **The Goal Success !**

You may choose to backup.
The Flexible opportunity may no longer exist.

Use your pencil to draw in an alternate risk path.
This takes you to the next step.
It's just another way to get there.

You may choose to quit.
That may involve risk (getting down from half-way up the mountain).
Draw the steps and use an eraser if the goal changes.

You may re-enter the main map at any point, including your goal.

An example is you may decide to park the car and fly to Cleveland.

About the Author

Daniel Stih

Pioneer, Innovator, Trailblazer

Daniel has climbed thirty mountains that had never been climbed. He has done the first ascents of ten mountains officially named on maps of Zion National Park (one of his favorite places to climb), more than any climber in history. Those include the Altar of Sacrifice, Sun Dial, Gregory Butte, the Bishopric(s), Abraham, Meridian Tower, Inclined Temple, Ivins Mountain, Castle Dome, and Cliff Dwelling Mountain. A true believer in the spirit of adventure and leaving no trace, most of his climbs do not have bolts (anchors).

He has a degree in Aerospace Engineering and worked at Motorola Inc..

Visit DanielStih.com or call (505) 603-8101 to inquire about booking him to speak or hiring him as a thought partner, or to suggest a guest for one of his podcasts.